INDUSTRY STANDARDS:
Network Marketing
Terms, Definitions, and Glossary

By:

Ryan Daley

Alpine, Utah, USA

ISBN 978-1456432324

Printed in the United States of America.

Cover Art supported by Wordle.net

PREFACE

One of the most common issues being an Industry Analyst within Network Marketing (early in my career), had been the erroneous use of terms within the industry in an effort to market or hype concepts as unique or different. This had been particularly annoying when nothing unique or different existed within the concept but a new word to say it with.

It wasn't until my very first major consulting job for a new start-up company that I learned how severely the use of common terms could be abused, risking both sides of the Network Marketing table (Distributor and Corporate).

I had been helping them to develop and audit a new compensation plan, and we had reached a point of discussing the branding and marketing of that compensation plan. Having been a respected Industry Analyst in the industry, and previously commissioned with the technical documents, I drafted the proposed technical marketing documents and submitted them for review to the Executive Team. When I received their personalized edits, and noticed that they had changed some of the terms erroneously, I requested a meeting with them to help clarify what the terms they were using meant. In my meeting with them, I used the example of Compression, and explained the type of Compression that was being programmed, and then the difference between that and the term of Compression that they were using. There was a significant difference to the Distributor between the two. The response back from them was that the term they wanted to use, even though they identified that it was not what people would expect, sounded better; it was more marketable – despite being wrong. They informed me that there were no official industry standards and that there was nothing wrong with branding the term different than its usual standard use in the industry, "Distributors don't know enough to challenge, and no entity is commissioned to govern these types of things."

At that point I became determined to do two things: (1) not renew my consulting agreement with them, and (2) help the industry create those standards to educate people in what to expect from the terms that are so commonly used (and misused) within the industry.

This story has a unique ending that helps to show the second edge of this sword. After about a year, I was talking with one of their Master Distributors, who was intimately aware of the previously described conversation. He mentioned to me that because of the documentation that the company distributed, the commission engine programmers took notice of it, and assumed that the company wanted programmed what they had seen issued to the Distributor Field, including the compression term that was used by the Executives. As a result, the programmers programmed the more marketable and expensive compression that was marketed by the company but never intended to actually go live.

Here is a perfect example of how a mix up or misuse of terms can not only effect and mislead the Distributor, but also directly affect the corporate environment and bottom line.

As the years have gone on, I have seen this become a growing problem in the industry, as more and more people become involved, one way or another, without any background or experience in the industry. This text also ended up taking much more time than I anticipated because of the breadth of research and experience needed to accurately capture these concepts with any degree of contextual comfort within the universal industry. I feel confident that I have been able to do so within human limitations; terms which have more than one potentially used definition are defined by the most common usage of the term, and terms with shared concepts have multiple explanations.

This text is designed to help bring unity to the terms that are used (and abused) within the industry. It is designed to be a reference for the novice who is just learning the industry, as well as the experienced who is trying to comprehend what other companies are trying to convey in their literature. This is to be a guidepost toward accurate documentation and minimizing marketing abuse and misuse within the industry (particularly the new entrants). And when all is said and done, it is to educate.

For those who have read my other texts, they know that my goals with all of my projects within the industry are to help refine the industry. To help the industry grow to the next level we must accept what has already been built as the foundation, and built upward from there; rather than regularly reinvent the foundation with every new company, trick, or concept.

I also understand the potential limitations within this ever expanding industry, and therefore refer the students of the industry to what I call "The Respectful Challenge." A few pages over, the reader will find an opportunity to help participate in this endeavor to standardize the industry and make this body of work more effective in its outlined goals.

I respectfully submit and offer this text to the industry. Enjoy, progress, and develop.

The Respectful Challenge

A text of this nature naturally had two characterizes: (1) that it will forever be incomplete, and (2) that it will always be challenged. These two facts bring a unique challenge to the author in keeping the text current and accurate. With that challenge in mind, the author welcomes the aforementioned characteristics.

Therefore, it is requested that in the circumstance where a definition is believed to be wrong or may need some correction, or that there is a term not included within this text that may be relevant to the industry – that the author is contacted immediately.

With the nature of this text and his publishing rights, the author has the ability to issue revised editions of this body of work regularly. Any comments, concerns, adjustments, or additional definitions are welcome, and should be submitted to the author for review.

All submissions should be sent to the author directly at daleyconsulting@gmail.com. Each submission should include the full name or business of the entity making the submissions, contact information, the requested submission or term, the proposed adjustment or definition, and their sources for the term (include relevant companies within the industry which use the term). The submission will then go through a research process to ensure that the term is indeed used in a fashion that constitutes an Industry Standard, and it will then be included within the next edition of the text. Please note, that the published term, after research and review, may not be exactly what was submitted but a more accurate view from a holistic industry perspective.

In addition to the term being included, the individual or entity which submitted the term to be added or corrected will be included at the back of the book with the acknowledgements for future editions. There are no royalties or rights issued for contributing suggestions or terms to the author and in turn being acknowledged.

Submissions, requests, and adjustments are welcomed and encouraged!

Dedicated to –
Gracie and Jude,
who are lavish with their love.

KEY

Within the definitions the reader will see words in SMALL CAPITALIZED LETTERS; this indicates that that word is a term which is defined within the body of work itself. The reader is encouraged if questions arise within definitions about terms used, to reference the capitalized terms within the book to gain greater insight and understanding. Terms capitalized within the text may not be exactly the same spelling as that defined, but finding the relevant definitions should be easy to manage (particularly in relation to plural terms).

A

ACTIVE (FOR BONUSES)- a status usually determined by QUALIFICATIONS within the COMPENSATION PLAN which allows the INDEPENDENT DISTRIBUTOR to earn some or all of their potential BONUSES or COMMISSIONS. Usually in order to be active for BONUSES requires the fulfillment of some basic QUALIFICATION; most commonly this is having placed an ORDER or accumulated an amount of volume within the month or the QUALIFICATION PERIOD, but may also include having a number of personally ENROLLED DISTRIBUTORS, or even having some small VOLUME requirements met within the SALES ORGANIZATION. Being active for bonuses, is usually the most rudimentary QUALIFICATIONS within the COMPENSATION PLAN RANK requirements; and AUTOSHIP is usually encouraged by the NETWORK MARKETING COMPANY as they easiest way to maintain that active status. Term is not to be confused with ACTIVE (FOR ORDERING). See also ORDER, RANKS, QUALIFICATIONS, BONUS, INACTIVE (FOR BONUSES), and COMMISSIONS.

ACTIVE (FOR ORDERING)- a status which indicates that an INDEPENDENT DISTRIBUTOR is not TERMINATED, CANCELLED, or SUSPENDED, and is in good standing with the company and therefore can order product, enroll new DISTRIBUTORS or CUSTOMERS, participate in the COMPENSATION PLAN, and access any of the services provided by the company without restriction. Each company may have different requirements to maintain an ACTIVE status within the COMPANY, and the consequences of losing ACTIVE status can also vary from company to company. Every NETWORK MARKETING COMPANY has guidelines established to determine who is ACTIVE (FOR ORDERING) within the ORGANIZATION in order to keep their costs down in account management, or to encourage a particular behavior to increase revenue or help cover the cost of account management. Some regularly used options for a company to identify whether an account remains ACTIVE (FOR ORDERING) are the following: whether the DISTRIBUTOR is up to date on all member or DISTRIBUTOR fees associated with the company, which may also include a RENEWAL FEE; whether the account holder has purchased COMMISSIONABLE PRODUCT within the a previous period of time (usually 6 to 12 months); whether they have personally accessed CUSTOMER SERVICE or their web based BACK OFFICE. All requirements for remaining ACTIVE (FOR ORDERING) are always detailed within each COMPANY'S POLICIES AND PROCEDURES, the neglect of which can deem the account INACTIVE and can require an additional cost in ordering or to reinstate ACTIVE status. Term is not to be confused with ACTIVE (FOR BONUSES). See also INACTIVE (FOR ORDERING), and POLICIES AND PROCEDURES.

APPLICATION- a form (either physical or electronic) used to request membership or status as a CUSTOMER, PREFERRED CUSTOMER, or INDEPENDENT DISTRIBUTOR for a NETWORK MARKETING COMPANY. APPLICATIONS require standard information from the applicant including, but not limited to: name, address, shipping information, birth date, desired initial ORDER, SPONSOR (or REFERRAL) information, etc. In the case of an APPLICATION for an INDEPENDENT

DISTRIBUTOR a Social Security Number or government Tax ID Number is required for tax purposes. APPLICATIONS are also usually paired up with a DISTRIBUTOR AGREEMENT, which is a legal document stating a number of immediate policies, Terms and Conditions, and refers the applicant to consult the POLICIES AND PROCEDURES. The application is also used as a legal document indicating the agreement to such POLICIES AND PROCEDURES, Terms and Conditions, any immediately pertinent policies, as well as the initial ORDER placed on the APPLICATION. See also ENROLLING

ASSOCIATE- a term used by some NETWORK MARKETING companies for an INDEPENDENT DISTRIBUTOR. These companies use this term in an effort to emphasis the relationships within the INDUSTRY between the INDEPENDENT DISTRIBUTORS and the NETWORK MARKETING COMPANY THEMSELVES. Refer to INDEPENDENT DISTRIBUTOR for full definition; also synonymous with INDEPENDENT BUSINESS OWNER (IBO), WHOLESALE DISTRIBUTOR, and INDEPENDENT PRODUCT CONSULTANT (IPC). See also DISTRIBUTOR.

ATTRITION - the rate, ratio, percentage, or timeline of the average active lifespan of an INDEPENDENT DISTRIBUTOR. Often used to refer to rate at which DISTRIBUTORS remove themselves from regular NETWORK MARKETING activities on behalf of a NETWORK MARKETING COMPANY, TEAM, or ORGANIZATION – and in relation to how quickly that inactivity takes place. The higher the ATTRITION rate, the more DISTRIBUTORS remove themselves from activity. ATTRITION is usually determined by the amount of DISTRIBUTORS that purchased one month (or CYCLE OF TIME to determine activity) but neglected to purchase the following month, in relation to the amount of active DISTRIBUTORS. ATTRITION means loss of sales or DISTRIBUTOR activity. See also RETENTION and INACTIVE (FOR BONUSES).

AUTOSHIP- a type of ORDER; particularly, where the DISTRIBUTOR agrees to have a standing reoccurring ORDER processed for PRODUCT or SERVICES every month or active CYCLE (PERIOD OF TIME); usually generated from an AUTOSHIP TEMPLATE. AUTOSHIPS can be part of some BONUS requirements within the COMPENSATION PLAN, but it is not necessarily internationally or domestically legal to require AUTOSHIPS for the majority of (or all) BONUSES within a COMPENSATION PLAN. AUTOSHIPS can also have minimum require- ments in relation to order size, or additional perks in relation to PRODUCT discounts, shipping discounts, or a reward point pro- gram towards free PRODUCT in an effort to incentivize AUTOSHIP ordering. AUTOSHIPS are traditionally the largest portion of any ORGANIZATION'S VOLUME or residual success. Although not legal in some countries and states, AUTOSHIP has at times been a re- quirement to being ACTIVE (FOR BONUSES), but can always be a requirement for a discount status, such as a PREFERRED CUSTOMER status or product discount. See also BUSINESS PROTECT (AUTOSHIP) and ORDER.

AUTOSHIP TEMPLATE- an unprocessed regular order invoice for product or services queued to be processed at a particular time or CYCLE (PERIOD OF TIME). An active or open AUTOSHIP TEMPLATE is usually set with the reoccurring date, desired PRODUCT, and payment method. Upon that date selected or predetermined by the NETWORK MARKETING COMPANY or the DISTRIBUTOR, the AUTOSHIP TEMPLATE will generate an ORDER with the preselected items and automatically pay the invoiced amount using the pre- selected payment method. See also AUTOSHIP.

B

Back Office- a web based secured site, where Independent Distributors will find tools to help them manage and build their business. Each network marketing company has different products, compensation plans, goals, and culture; therefore, each company also offered different tools to their Independent Distributors in an effort to help them grow their business to the best of their abilities. These tools, trainings, and other resources can usually be found in the Back Office provided by the company. Many companies also offer different back office packages with different tools for various fees. Each company should offer a basic Back Office to allow the Independent Distributor to view is Downline or Genealogy as well as identify any necessary information regarding his current or future earnings within the compensation plan, their team volumes, the ability to order product, manage their Autoships, and receive news or have access to copies of corporate agreements (Policies and Procedures, Distributor Applications, etc.). Term is often synonymous with Virtual Office.

Binary (Structure)- a compensation plan structure type that indicates that the placement of each new enrollment must be placed within one of two legs within an organization. The term binary refers to "two"; each position within the structure is allowed only two directly connected (placed) positions under them. This fact requires that many INDEPENDENT DISTRIBUTORS place newly SPONSORED DISTRIBUTORS within the ORGANIZATION or team of other INDEPENDENT DISTRIBUTORS – which creates the perception of team work and unity within the ORGANIZATION. There is no requirement that a DISTRIBUTOR must have two legs within the structure itself, although it often times is a requirement in order to qualify for a number of BONUSES; and no organization can have more than two legs in the BINARY TREE. Types of COMPENSATION PLAN models based off of BINARY structures include: CYCLE BINARY, WEAKER LEG BINARY, and HYBRID BINARY. See also STRUCTURE TYPE, UNILEVEL, and MATRIX.

BINARY BONUS- a BONUS within the COMPENSATION PLAN which pays off of the STRUCTURE, VOLUME, or DISTRIBUTOR ACTIVITY within the BINARY TREE of an INDEPENDENT DISTRIBUTOR. This can include BONUSES which pay specific to CYCLE BINARIES or WEAKER LEG BINARIES, and can often be titled under different marketed names. BINARY BONUSES can have requirements and QUALIFICATIONS within the BINARY STRUCTURE. The most common QUALIFICATION for a BINARY BONUS is often in relation to the number of personally ENROLLED ACTIVE (FOR BONUS) members within the BINARY TREE; usually with the requirement of having a number of personally ACTIVE (FOR BONUS) ENROLLMENTS within each LEG of the BINARY. This is usually considered a RESIDUAL BONUS of the COMPENSATION PLAN with a BINARY TREE attached. Other BONUSES based off of the STRUCTURE TYPE of the COMPENSATION PLAN are UNILEVEL BONUS and MATRIX BONUS. See also RECRUITING BONUS, FAST START BONUS, STRUCTURE BONUS, and MATCHING BONUS.

BINARY COMMISSIONS- refers to the EARNINGS or COMMISSIONS of an INDEPENDENT DISTRIBUTOR which is earned from any BINARY BONUSES that were QUALIFIED for and offered within the COMPENSATION PLAN. This can commonly be referred to as a RESIDUAL COMMISSION; similar to UNILEVEL COMMISSIONS and MATRIX COMMISSIONS. See also COMMISSIONS, EARNINGS, and COMMISSION PAYMENTS.

BINARY LEGS- refers to the two TEAMS that each DISTRIBUTOR is required to build within a BINARY STRUCTURE. As each BINARY only allows two direct PLACEMENTS to each DISTRIBUTOR, this creates two LEGS for the INDEPENDENT DISTRIBUTOR and therefore their BINARY LEGS. These two LEGS are usually titled the RIGHT LEG (or TEAM) and the LEFT LEG (or TEAM) – identified by as if the DISTRIBUTOR was looking at their ORGANIZATION on a board, not as if they are looking down their ORGANIZATION. As a result of the BINARY STRUCTURE one LEG is inherently directly shared with the upline, known as the COMMON LEG; the opposite leg is the UNCOMMON LEG. See also LEGS.

BINARY LEG VOLUME- the total amount of accumulated VOLUME that has been generated, purchased, bought, or sold by the members of the ORGANIZATION within a particulate LEG of the DISTRIBUTORS BINARY STRUCTURE for a given COMMISSION or QUALIFICATION PERIOD. This is the grand total of all the VOLUME within a particular LEG of the BINARY TREE, and is often used directly in the calculation of any BINARY BONUSES within the published COMPENSATION PLAN.

BINARY TREE- TREE which details the genealogical or PLACEMENT relationship of ENROLLMENTS or PLACEMENTS within the confines of a BINARY STRUCTURE. Often BINARY TREES only refer to the PLACEMENT (not the enrollment) of the distributors within an ORGANIZATION; and therefore officially classified as a PLACEMENT TREE. As with the nature of the BINARY structure, the BINARY TREE details the structure of only two LEGS of the DISTRIBUTOR'S ORGANIZATION. Usually, new ENROLLMENTS are placed within one of two teams or LEGS within the BINARY TREE. The main units of consideration within the BINARY TREE are: (1) LEG VOLUME, (2) its relationship and comparison with the opposing LEG of the BINARY structure, (3) and the PLACEMENT of team member between one of the two teams. Each BINARY TREE is allowed to have two LEGS or teams (RIGHT LEG or LEFT LEG) and unlimited LEVELS of depth. BINARY BONUSES are determined by the VOLUME and activity within the BINARY TREE. See also TREE, UNILEVEL TREE, ENROLLMENT TREE, SPONSOR TREE, and MATRIX TREE.

BINARY TREE VOLUME- the amount of total PRODUCT VOLUME accumulated throughout the entire BINARY TREE ORGANIZATION within a given COMMISSION or QUALIFICATION PERIOD. This VOLUME sums the VOLUMES within both BINARY LEGS. This can also refer to ORGANIZATION VOLUME within the respective BINARY STRUCTURE.

BONUS- a COMMISSION model within a COMPENSATION PLAN designed to compensate an INDEPENDENT DISTRIBUTOR for a particular behavior or activity. BONUSES all carry with them QUALIFICATIONS or REQUIREMENTS in order to earn a predetermined COMMISSION as detailed within the COMPANY'S published COMPENSATION PLAN. BONUSES are earned through activity that is incentivize by the NETWORK MARKETING COMPANY, and are generated from the COMMISSIONABLE SALES VOLUME accumulated within a particular COMMISSION PERIOD. BONUSES generate COMMISSIONS which in turn

PRODUCT an Independent Distributor earnings. Bonuses can be qualified for as a result of activity, and still might not generate commissions as a result of the lack of commissionable sales volume within the boundaries or nature of the particular bonus. Examples of Bonuses are: Binary Bonus, Unilevel Bonus, Matrix Bonus, Cycle (Unit of Volume,) PayGate, Override, Retail Bonus (or Commissions), Matching Bonus, Leadership Bonus, Bonus Pools, and Fast Start Bonus. See also Residual Bonuses.

Bonus Buying- a standard policy violation usually detailed within a company's published Policies and Procedures. This refers to when an Independent Distributor identifies the potential to increase in rank or qualify for a bonus that would increase their commission earnings or payments, and subsequently purchases additional volume personally but placed within the organization in an attempt to qualify for said bonus. This violation indicates that the Independent Distributor for all intents and purposes purchased or bought their own way into that qualification or rank in turn buying their bonus or recognition; in contrast the Independent Distributor is encourages to enroll, retain, or legitimately improve sales within their organization to qualify for said bonuses. The results of this action often times increases their own check, yet with the nature of many compensation plans decrease the potential earnings of unrelated Distributors within the company, and in essence it considered using manipulation to steal from the company or other distributors using the compensation plan. This violation is usually identified by the Commission Department, and enforced by the Compliance Department within the corporate environment. Usual results or actions taken by a network marketing company that has identified such actions or behaviors can include retraction of earnings,

SUSPENSION, TERMINATION, and in severe cases external legal recourse. Violations are usually identified by the use of similar credit cards and similar shipping addresses on multiple ORDERS (with addresses being the single most common identifying marker), or perfectly build ORGANIZATIONS. See also COMMISSION MANIPULATION, STACKING, and CROSS RECRUITING.

BONUS POOLS- BONUS where there is an accumulation of funds which are pooled together from a part, portion, or the whole of SALES and then divided out among qualified participants. QUALIFICATIONS are usually determined within the COMPENSATION PLAN literature, and the funds are usually collected through a percentage of COMMISSIONABLE VOLUME generated within a COMPANY or ORGANIZATION, otherwise known as TOTAL COMPANY COMMISSIONABLE VOLUME. Funds can be issued through shares that are collected and then share values determined in relation to the funds pooled and the amount of shares earned within the COMPANY. BONUS POOL earnings can be affected by the amount of people qualified for the POOL, the amount of funds collected for the POOL, or the amount of total shares issued for the POOL. See also LEADERSHIP POOL.

BONUS VOLUME (BV)- synonymous with COMMISSIONABLE VOLUME (CV). Please see COMMISSIONABLE VOLUME for a full definition.

BREAKAGE- a term used to describe the difference between what a NETWORK MARKETING COMPANY declares, markets, or proposes they *can* or will pay in COMMISSIONS through their published COMPENSATION PLAN and what they *actually* pay in COMMISSIONS to their INDEPENDENT DISTRIBUTORS. The amount that a NETWORK MARKETING COMPANY claims they pay is usually what they could pay or have the potential to pay, if everything was QUALIFIED for within the COMPENSATION PLAN. In most circumstances where there is BREAKAGE is it a result of money that was not QUALIFIED for and therefore was not paid out to the DISTRIBUTOR field; and in most of these circumstances where BREAKAGE exists within a COMPANY'S COMPENSATION PLAN it is also intended to exist in an attempt to keep cash flow and equity higher within the COMPANY. BREAKAGE can also be created intentionally by the COMPANY as a result of COMMISSION MANIPULATION from inside the COMPANY through CORPORATE owned positions, or impossible to qualify for BONUSES where the potential COMMISSIONS are not reallocated to other BONUSES or PROMOTIONS. The NETWORK MARKETING COMPANY'S CORPORATE environment and EXECUTIVE TEAM have full control and power as to how much BREAKAGE exists and does not exist within the COMPANY'S COMPENSATION PLAN. The less BREAKAGE a COMPANY has the less money the COMPANY keeps and more money is sent out to the DISTRIBUTOR FIELD. The more BREAKAGE that a COMPANY has the more money the COMPANY retains that they marketed would be paid out to the DISTRIBUTOR field that is not being issued out in the form of COMMISSIONS or EARNINGS. BREAKAGE is a not openly discussed by any NETWORK MARKETING COMPANY, unless they are comfortable with their attempt to minimize it for the benefit of the DISTRIBUTOR FIELD. Yet, it should be noted that in many circumstances even with claims of minimized BREAKAGE, the COMPANY can still be creating, accepting, and intending the recapture of BREAKAGE through the COMPENSATION PLAN; and it takes a very well trained eye to be able to identify the potential of BREAKAGE within a COMPANY. In short, BREAKAGE is money that (as described by the COMPANY itself) should be going to the DISTRIBUTOR, but is really going back to the COMPANY (often with full intention and acceptance thereof).

BUSINESS PROTECT (AUTOSHIP)- a type of ORDER or AUTOSHIP TEMPLATE; particularly, where the DISTRIBUTOR agrees to have a potential standing ORDER processed for PRODUCT or SERVICES in the event that within a month or an ACTIVE CYCLE (PERIOD OF TIME) a regular ORDER has not been processed for the purposes of qualifying for a bonus within the COMPENSATION PLAN or PROMOTION. BUSINESS PROTECT AUTOSHIPS only process when no other ORDER has been placed to fill any requirements that may be present within the COMPANY COMPENSATION PLAN or BONUS. See also AUTOSHIP and ORDER.

C

CALL CENTER- the location or department where inbound and outbound customer service oriented calls are received, managed, and handled for the CORPORATE NETWORK MARKETING COMPANY. Term can be synonymous with or include the following departments: DISTRIBUTOR NETWORK SERVICES, CUSTOMER SERVICE DEPARTMENT, and ORDER ENTRY DEPARTMENT. See also ELITE SERVICES and LEADERSHIP SERVICES.

CANCELLATION- the act of an INDEPENDENT DISTRIBUTOR to voluntarily request or demand the CANCELLATION of their account with the NETWORK MARKETING COMPANY; and therefore, opts out of participating in any AUTOSHIP PROGRAMS, building activity, or claiming any future COMMISSION EARNINGS. The completion of canceling an account yields the account as TERMINATED, and places the account in an INACTIVE (FOR ORDERING) status. As a result of potential manipulation, most companies through their POLICIES AND PROCEDURES require that the canceling DISTRIBUTOR to physically submit a signed or notarized letter requesting the action. See also SUSPENDED, TERMINATED, and ACTIVE (FOR ORDERING).

CAP- the most amount of money or COMMISSIONS that may be issued, earned, or distributed. CAPS can be directly associated with the most a BONUS can pay as a whole, the most a COMPENSATION PLAN can distribute as a whole, or the most an INDEPENDENT DISTRIBUTOR can earn from a BONUS or from the COMPENSATION PLAN individually. CAPS are often used to stabilize a COMPENSATION PLAN, and to aid in creating and incentivizing a particular behavior. All COMPENSATION PLANS are CAPPED whether through their inherent STRUCTURE, or through a directly stated CAP. Term is often synonymous with EARNING POTENTIAL.

CARRY FORWARD VOLUME – term is synonymous with CARRY OVER VOLUME. Please refer to CARRY OVER VOLUME for the full definition.

CARRY OVER VOLUME- refers to VOLUME that was accumulated within one COMMISSION or QUALIFICATION PERIOD that is moved into the proceeding PERIOD. This usually refers to VOLUME that was accumulated within an ORGANIZATION but that was not COMMISSIONED on, and was therefore carried over into the next PERIOD to be used later (pending QUALIFICATIONS). Often times this is seen in BINARY STRUCTURES, when one LEG is unbalanced and therefore contains more VOLUME than will be paid on in the

BINARY BONUS; that VOLUME may carry forward to help the ORGANIZATION for the future week. In most circumstances in order to have CARRY OVER VOLUME accumulate, the COMPANY will have QUALIFICATIONS - most commonly the need to remain ACTIVE (FOR BONUSES). CARRY OVER VOLUME allows the INDEPENDENT DISTRIBUTOR to not lose any VOLUME that may result in an unbalanced ORGANIZATION, but allow any unpaid VOLUME to be carried forward to potentially be paid out in the future. CARRY OVER VOLUME is a necessary program in all COMPENSATION PLANS that use a BINARY STRUCTURE in conjunction with a WEEKLY COMMISSION or QUALIFICATION CYCLE – in order to even function as a VOLUME STRUCTURE. In circumstances where any QUALIFICATIONS are not consistently met CARRY OVER VOLUME may be flushed and removed from the account. See also FLUSHED VOLUME.

CENTER LEG (MATRIX)- refers to the LEG in a MATRIX structure that is not the far RIGHT LEG or LEFT LEG (OUTSIDE LEGS) of the ORGANIZATION. A CENTER LEG is the LEG or ORGANIZATION that is in between the LEFT and RIGHT STRUCTURES, and is therefore inherently an UNCOMMON LEG. See also RIGHT LEG (MATRIX) and LEFT LEG (MATRIX).

CHECK- a method of being paid or paying COMMISSIONS or EARNINGS through a bank backed check issued by the NETWORK MARKETING COMPANY. This is the most common method of payment used in NETWORK MARKETING. See also DIRECT DEPOSIT, PAY CARD, and eWALLET.

CHILD- term can refer to a DOWNLINE member or personally SPONSORED DISTRIBUTOR of another DISTRIBUTOR. Term is usually used in the INDUSTRY to denote a relationship of protégé and

14

training from the PARENT DISTRIBUTOR. See also PARENT, SPONSOR, UPLINE, and DOWNLINE.

COLD MARKET- a term used in NETWORK MARKETING to denote a population of people or potential future RECRUITS in which there is no previous association or relationship with a specific INDEPENDENT DISTRIBUTOR. These are referred to cold relationships, as there wasn't previously a relationship there to build upon in an effort to market the PRODUCT or OPPORTUNITY which the NETWORK MARKETING COMPANY offers. Developing COLD MARKET LEADS directs people to contact those whom they previously were not aware of or had any previous relationship with. This is opposed to a WARM MARKET.

COMMISSIONABLE PRODUCT- PRODUCT or SERVICES in which a portion of the SALES is issued to UPLINE members of the TREE ORGANIZATION in the form of COMMISSIONABLE VOLUME or QUALIFYING VOLUME with the intention of generating COMMISSIONS or EARNINGS. This term indicates that the PRODUCT is qualified to generate COMMISSIONS for TEAM members within an ORGANIZATION pending the successful SALE or transaction of such product. See also UNCOMMISSIONABLE PRODUCT.

COMMISSIONABLE VOLUME (CV)- a type of VOLUME that indicates the amount of credit from the purchase or sale of a PRODUCT or SERVICE that is considered to be commissionable. COMMISSIONABLE VOLUME is the VOLUME amount that the COMMISSIONS are calculated from within the COMMISSION ENGINE. There are times when the COMMISSIONABLE VOLUME, and the SALES VOLUME are equal, at which point COMMISSIONABLE VOLUME usually isn't identified as a VOLUME type; but it is not uncommon for the actual EARNINGS generated from a BONUS in the COMPENSATION PLAN is generated from a VOLUME amount that is different than the SALES VOLUME. COMMISSIONABLE VOLUME can also be viewed as a currency type for the COMMISSION ENGINE to calculate COMMISSIONS. COMMISSIONABLE VOLUME is the only number that the COMMISSION ENGINE uses to calculate the EARNINGS from each BONUS within the COMPENSATION PLAN. There are times with some COMPENSATION PLAN when published COMMISSIONABLE VOLUME is discounted for a PERIOD of time as a result of a FAST START BONUS paying out the majority of the available funds from the purchase of that PRODUCT. In circumstances where COMMISSIONABLE VOLUME is not published it is usually a result of the PRODUCT VOLUME amount is equal to the COMMISSIONABLE VOLUME amount that is calculated in the COMMISSION ENGINE – and therefore only PRODUCT VOLUME would be publically marketed. See also PERSONAL VOLUME, PRODUCT VOLUME, QUALIFYING VOLUME, SALES VOLUME, and UNCOMMISSIONABLE VOLUME.

COMMISSION DEPARTMENT- a department within the CORPORATE ENVIRONMENT which manages and maintains the COMMISSION ENGINE, audits COMMISSION PAYOUTS, and manages COMMISSION PAYMENT METHODS (CHECK, PAY CARD, eWALLET, DIRECT DEPOSIT, etc.). Often times the COMMISSION DEPARTMENT will also manage COMPENSATION PLAN material, trainings both within the CORPORATE ENVIRONMENT as well as within the DISTRIBUTOR FIELD, and completes competitive analysis for the EXECUTIVE team members. See also MARKETING DEPARTMENT, DISTRIBUTOR NETWORK SERVICES, SALE DEPARTMENT, and ELITE SERVICES.

COMMISSION ENGINE- a dynamic program within a secure environment hosted by a software package, which contains the

COMPENSATION PLAN programming to generate all of the COMMISSION calculations and RANK QUALIFICATIONS as a result of VOLUME and QUALIFICATIONS which are accumulated within a particular COMMISSION or QUALIFICATION PERIOD. The COMMISSION ENGINE contains the full logic of the published COMPENSATION PLAN of the NETWORK MARKETING COMPANY, and is directly tied to the data which creates and monitors the TREE VOLUME and ORGANIZATION. The COMMISSION ENGINE is usually ran, audited, and maintained by the COMMISSION DEPARTMENT within the CORPORATE ENVIRONMENT.

COMMISSION MANIPULATION- usually a strict policy violation involving the attempt to adjust VOLUME or an ORGANIZATION fraudulently in an effort to maximize an INDEPENDENT DISTRIBUTOR'S COMMISSION EARNINGS which they would not have earned otherwise. Within the company's PUBLISHED POLICIES AND PROCEDURES there are usually a number of policies and consequences documented in an effort to minimize or enforce such violations. There are many ways COMMISSION MANIPULATION can be attempted, the most common ones are usually documented within the NETWORK MARKETING COMPANIES POLICIES AND PROCEDURES but because of changing trend there are usually generic polices around COMMISSION MANIPULATION as deemed appropriate or enforceable by the company. COMMISSION MANIPULATION is usually identified by the COMMISSION DEPARTMENT, but monitored and enforced by the COMPLIANCE DEPARTMENT. Often types this term can be synonymous with BONUS BUYING and STACKING.

COMMISSION PAYMENT- the paying of COMMISSIONS that have been earned through the NETWORK MARKETING COMPANY'S COMPENSATION PLAN as calculated by the COMPANY'S COMMISSION ENGINE, and generated as a result of DOWNLINE PRODUCT SALES or VOLUME accumulation. COMMISSION PAYMENTS are paid to INDEPENDENT DISTRIBUTORS through various methods, such as: CHECK, DIRECT DEPOSIT, EWALLET, and PAY CARD.

COMMISSION PERIOD- PERIOD of time pre-determined by the COMPANY in which VOLUME and STRUCTURE of an ORGANIZATION are taken into consideration within the COMMISSION ENGINE for consideration determination of COMMISSIONS for a particular payout schedule. This PERIOD is usually in between two dates and can be a calendar month, calendar week, or any other PERIOD of time as determined and marketed by the COMPANY. Only VOLUME generated within the COMMISSION PERIOD is calculated in COMMISSION ENGINE for a COMMISSION run. COMMISSION PERIODS are often ran simultaneously with QUALIFICATION PERIODS.

COMMISSIONS- refer to the amount of EARNINGS issued to an INDEPENDENT DISTRIBUTOR as a result of the activity or SALES within in SALES ORGANIZATION. This can also be a more general term which refers to all the funds issued in the form of BONUS EARNINGS from a company to the respective DISTRIBUTOR FIELD. COMMISSIONS are earned and calculated in accordance with the published COMPENSATION PLAN of the NETWORK MARKETING COMPANY, and are always considered taxable earnings. COMMISSION payout is usually also subject to adherence to the companies published POLICIES AND PROCEDURES. See also BONUSES and EARNINGS.

COMMON LEG- this is the LEG that is directly shared with an UPLINE SPONSOR or PLACEMENT. This term is most commonly relevant within BINARY or MATRIX structures. This is the LEG or TEAM that an UPLINE is most likely to support or build naturally because of the PLACEMENT relationship between an UPLINE member and the INDEPENDENT DISTRIBUTOR. For example: if the DISTRIBUTOR is placed within the LEFT LEG of the UPLINE PLACEMENT, when that UPLINE PLACEMENT is going to place new members within his LEFT LEG, they naturally will look first at continuing to build the LEFT portion of that LEG and in turn build the LEFT team of the INDEPENDENT DISTRIBUTOR. This would indicate that the LEFT leg in this circumstance is the COMMON LEG; the LEG of an ORGANIZATION that is shared with the direct UPLINE member, and that they are more than likely to directly build naturally; the LEG within an ORGANIZATION that naturally is going to be commonly shared in relation to the building process of the ORGANIZATION. OUTSIDE LEGS are also commonly referred to as a COMMON LEG. All other LEGS in the organization would be considered an UNCOMMON LEG.

COMPANY- refers to the NETWORK MARKETING COMPANY as a whole, meaning the specific institution; including the corporate staff, PRODUCT, CULTURE, MARKETING, and COMPENSATION PLAN. See also NETWORK MARKETING COMPANY.

COMPENSATION PLAN- the advertised marketing plan which details the rules and processes which govern how an INDEPENDENT DISTRIBUTOR can expect to earn COMMISSIONS on the SALES generated within their organization. COMPENSATION PLANS are created with the intention to generate sales behavior and incentive activity through the BONUSES that comprise the plan. COMPENSATION PLANS can also detail the intended programming within the COMMISSION ENGINE, and what logic the engine will use to generate the DISTRIBUTORS EARNINGS. COMPENSATION PLANS can also detail other benefits, goals, and objectives of DISTRIBUTORS or the CORPORATE ENVIRONMENT. RANKS, RANK QUALIFICATIONS, and

LIMITATIONS are also often detailed in the COMPENSATION PLAN. This term is a synonymous with COMMISSION PLAN. See also BONUSES.

COMPLIANCE DEPARTMENT- department within the NETWORK MARKETING CORPORATE ENVIRONMENT which manages the task of legally protecting the corporation and the DISTRIBUTOR FIELD. The COMPLIANCE DEPARTMENT usually monitors claims, allegations, or activity of the DISTRIBUTOR field in order to protect the corporation from legal liabilities from government entities such as State Attorney Generals, the Food and Drug Administration, and the Federal Trade Commission. Claims, allegations, or activity that is monitored may include: health claims in relation to the product, financial claims in relation to the COMPENSATION PLAN, false claims in relation to supporters or funders of the COMPANY, or the use of official corporate material to minimize false impressions. This department also manages requests in relation to changes within the ORGANIZATION or any actions, requests, or behavior that may be governed by the POLICIES AND PROCEDURES. For other departments within the CORPORATE ENVIRONMENT see also CUSTOMER SERVICE, MARKETING DEPARTMENT, SALES DEPARTMENT, and the EXECUTIVE TEAM.

COMPRESSION- the way in which a COMMISSION ENGINE compensates for INACTIVE positions within an ORGANIZATION TREE for the purpose of COMMISSION EARNINGS and QUALIFICATIONS. Often times within the building of an ORGANIZATION TREE or GENEALOGY INACTIVE positions within a COMMISSION or QUALIFICATION PERIOD will exist. These positions are INACTIVE due to the lack of a COMMISSIONABLE order, or check qualifying (as determined by the COMPENSATION PLAN). In these circumstances these positions can hinder the calculation of COMMISSION EARNINGS, as these INACTIVE positions may take up a LEVEL or spot which generates zero COMMISSIONS for the UPLINE and hampers the EARNINGS of COMMISSIONS on deeper VOLUME or LEVELS. COMPRESSION is necessary (particularly within UNILEVEL plans) to help the DISTRIBUTOR overcome or COMPENSATION for these INACTIVE positions. The way in which COMPRESSION is calculated can be varied in regard to the type of COMPRESSION that the company offers. Types of COMPRESSION include: STANDARD COMPRESSION, DYNAMIC COMPRESSION (ORIGINAL), and DYNAMIC COMPRESSION (COMPRESSED). Other forms of COMPRESSION that are less identified as just would be: GENERATIONS, OVERRIDE COMPRESSION, and ROLL-UP VOLUME.

CONFERENCE CALL- a tool used by DISTRIBUTORS in which a training or recruiting meeting is conducted via the telephone with multiple attendees, invitees, or listeners. See also WEBINAR.

CONVENTION- often times is the largest CORPORATE sponsored EVENT within a year for the DISTRIBUTOR FIELD. CONVENTION is the ultimate CORPORATE meeting which usually can include exclusive offers for attendees, new PRODUCT launches, business building trainings, PRODUCT trainings, PARTIES, and TEAM socializing. CONVENTION also is traditionally the largest show of recognition for DISTRIBUTOR achievements throughout the year.

CORPORATE ENVIRONMENT- refers to the EXECUTIVE team, structure, and corporate CULTURE within the corporate offices of the NETWORK MARKETING COMPANY and is the total sum or constitution of all included Departments. Included corporate departments which make the CORPORATE ENVIRONMENTS include, but are not limited to: COMMISSIONS DEPARTMENT, CUSTOMER SERVICE, DISTRIBUTOR NETWORK SERVICES, ORDER ENTRY, ELITE OR LEADERSHIP

SERVICES, EXECUTIVE TEAM, MARKETING DEPARTMENT, SALES DEPARTMENT, and an Accounting of Finance Department. This environment is credited to developing or being the foundation for the DISTRIBUTOR FIELD and CULTURE that is established among the DISTRIBUTORS. The CORPORATE ENVIRONMENT as a whole is also credited for developing strategic direction and its implementation. The CORPORATE ENVIRONMENT in often times referred to in contrast to the FIELD which is composed of DISTRIBUTORS; as the CORPORATE ENVIRONMENT represents the COMPANY as a whole, the field represents that distributor representation of the NETWORK MARKETING COMPANY.

CROSS RECRUITING- usually a violation of policy documented within the COMPANY'S published POLICIES AND PROCEDURES, which includes the attempted or successful solicitation of one INDEPENDENT DISTRIBUTOR to another INDEPENDENT DISTRIBUTOR of the same NETWORK MARKETING COMPANY to another ORGANIZATION or position in the TREE. That other ORGANIZATION can include another DISTRIBUTOR TEAM within the same COMPANY or to a new NETWORK MARKETING COMPANY. CROSS RECRUITING is the most policed policy in regard to the POLICIES AND PROCEDURES, as it has the largest potential to affect the business of tens, hundreds, or thousands of similar DISTRIBUTOR businesses. In most circumstances it is not considered CROSS RECRUITING if the solicitation is issued by the personal ENROLLER of the DISTRIBUTOR; but if there is no direct ENROLLMENT relationship (not just through the ENROLLMENT TREE) than it will be officially considered CROSS RECRUITING and is full enforceable. CROSS RECRUITING within the same COMPANY, from one position in the TREE to another position in the TREE, is highly enforced or monitored within the COMPANY to protect the DISTRIBUTOR businesses that may be affected. CROSS RECRUITING from one NETWORK MARKETING COMPANY to another NETWORK MARKETING COMPANY is strictly enforced, monitored, and policed, as it not only directly effects the DISTRIBUTOR businesses within the COMPANY but the bottom line of the COMPANY as well; this type of CROSS RECRUITING is not only enforced by policy but is regularly taken to court or becomes a legal issue very quickly.

CULTURE- a broad terms used to denote the many aspects of an ORGANIZATION's behavior. CULTURE usually refers to the behavior that is seen within the NETWORK MARKETING COMPANY'S DISTRIBUTOR FIELD: purchasing patterns, event activities, RECOGNITION, ENROLLMENT and recruitment strategies, etc. CULTURE can be fostered and encouraged by the CORPORATE ENVIRONMENT through the MARKETING DEPARTMENT and the SALES DEPARTMENT – but very often it is an outgrowth of the LEADING DISTRIBUTOR's behavior or success.

CUSTOMER – a CUSTOMER TYPE that identifies the individual as a RETAIL purchaser of the NETWORK MARKETING COMPANY'S PRODUCTS or SERVICES. CUSTOMERS do not participate in the COMPENSATION PLAN or any other NETWORK MARKETING activities, but only purchase PRODUCT at the full RETAIL PRICE either directly from the COMPANY or from other INDEPENDENT DISTRIBUTORS. CUSTOMERS who pur-chase directly from the COMPANY must submit an application. CUSTOMER purchases often also reflect as the direct purchases of the referring or SPONSORING DISTRIBUTOR. Term is synonymous with RETAIL CUSTOMER. See also DISTRIBUTOR and PREFERRED CUSTOMER.

CUSTOMER SERVICE DEPARTMENT- a department within the CORPORATE ENVIRONMENT given the task to service the DISTRIBUTOR'S needs and support them in developing and growing their own business. CUSTOMER SERVICE DEPARTMENT can be an all inclusive title for the CALL CENTER, but very often is also a separate department within the CALL CENTER, with the ORDER ENTRY DEPARTMENT and ELITE or LEADERSHIP SERVICES being separate with a different call queue for quicker orders and servicing. The CUSTOMER SERVICE DEPARTMENT can perform tasks that can include and may not be limited to: ordering, COMMISSIONS challenges, returning products (issuing RMAs), asking general COMPANY and INDUSTRY questions, and providing any service that is reasonable and requested by the DISTRIBUTOR or RETAIL CUSTOMER. See also DISTRIBUTOR NETWORK SERVICES (DNS).

CUSTOMER TYPE- categorizes the different purchasing members of the NETWORK MARKETING COMPANY. All individuals who purchase from a NETWORK MARKETING COMPANY are categorized within different CUSTOMER TYPES or categories. Usually there are three CUSTOMER TYPES: DISTRIBUTOR, CUSTOMER, and PREFERRED CUSTOMER. Each of these CUSTOMER TYPES has different activities which define them in their respective category. Refer to DISTRIBUTOR, CUSTOMER, and PREFERRED CUSTOMER to identify what activities define each CUSTOMER TYPE.

CYCLE (UNIT OF TIME)- calendar unit used to determine QUALIFICATION PERIODS in which the INDEPENDENT DISTRIBUTOR can expect to have within a COMMISSION PERIOD to build towards QUALIFICATIONS, RANKS, and COMMISSIONS. CYCLES are usually determined with the nature of the COMPENSATION PLAN, and can be in relation to COMMISSION PERIOD, or the length of time an INDEPENDENT DISTRIBUTOR is considered ACTIVE (FOR BONUSES) within the COMPANY'S COMPENSATION PLAN. CYCLES for COMMISSION or QUALIFICATION PERIODS are determined by how often the

COMMISSIONS are processed and determined; this can include the PERIOD in which the VOLUME accumulates within an ORGANIZATION at the point at which it is paid and the VOLUME then flushed. Examples of CYCLES for COMMISSIONS or QUALIFICATION PERIODS are: yearly, monthly, weekly, and sometimes within real-time. CYCLES related to being ACTIVE (FOR BONUSES) are determined by the amount of time an INDEPENDENT DISTRIBUTOR is expected to order regularly (or accumulated PERSONAL VOLUME) while maintain the expectation within the documented COMPENSATION PLAN to earn any or all COMMISSIONS offered by the COMPANY. Examples related to being ACTIVE (FOR BONUSES) are: monthly, every four weeks, bi-weekly, or weekly. CYCLES related to COMMISSION PERIODS or QUALIFICATIONS are usually connected directly with the CYCLES related to ACTIVE (FOR BONUSES) with a few exceptions. Monthly CYCLES usually pay COMMISSIONS every month, but also only require an order or accumulated PERSONAL VOLUME ever month. One exception that still has a relationship between the two but not as direct: plans that allow for weekly paid COMMISSIONS for their basic residual income often will only require an order or the accumulation of PERSONAL VOLUME every four weeks or bi-weekly; that four week QUALIFICATION would be considered a CYCLE (UNIT OF TIME).

CYCLE (UNIT OF VOLUME)- unit used within CYCLE BINARIES to determine the primary RESIDUAL COMMISSIONS. A CYCLE is determined by having a predetermined about of VOLUME in each LEG; or in other words, VOLUME between the two LEGS in the form of a ratio of VOLUME. The COMPANY predetermines what VOLUME relationship determined a "CYCLE", and the company also predetermines the value of each CYCLE produced. There can be and should be multiple CYCLES within each ORGANIZATION as it grows. CYCLES are usually describe in the format of XXX/YYY, indicating that for each CYCLE to be complete there needs to be XXX VOLUME unused volume in one LEG, while there is YYY VOLUME of unused VOLUME in the opposite LEG. Once VOLUME is associated with a CYCLE, the CYCLE is filled, and the CYCLE is paid for; the VOLUME is then considered used, and is FLUSHED.

CYCLE BINARY- a COMPENSATION PLAN model using the BINARY STRUCTURE TYPE; COMPENSATION is generally determined in relation to the number of CYCLES (UNITS OF VOLUME), or accumulation of VOLUME into units, created when comparing each LEG of the BINARY structure. CYCLE BINARIES pay a predetermined COMMISSION per CYCLE (UNITS OF VOLUME) generated within the ORGANIZATION. The more CYCLES (UNITS OF VOLUME) generated within the BINARY ORGANIZATION, the more COMMISSIONS are earned from the ORGANIZATION. CYCLE BINARIES often are used to allow an unbalanced perspective between the two LEGS, allowing there to be more or less in one LEG than in the other LEG in order to create a cycle (UNIT OF VOLUME). When a CYCLE is calculated and paid the VOLUME used to create that CYCLE is then FLUSHED, or removed from the tree. CYCLE BINARIES are inherently unstable for the long run, and usually are only used for a short period of time before adjustment is enforced by the COMPANY. Other types of COMPENSATION PLAN models from the BINARY STRUCTURE TYPE are: HYBRID BINARY and WEAK LEG BINARY.

D

DIRECT DEPOSIT- a method of being paid or paying COMMISSIONS or EARNINGS from a NETWORK MARKETING COMPANY through a bank transfer or directly depositing COMMISSIONS or EARNINGS into a bank account of the DISTRIBUTOR'S choice (checking or savings). This is the most sought after method in NETWORK MARKETING, as it decreases delivery time of payment for the DISTRIBUTOR and minimized company overhead costs. See also CHECK, PAY CARD, and EWALLET.

DIRECT PRODUCT- see "PRODUCT" for definition. See also INDIRECT PRODUCT.

DIRECT SALES- term can be synonymous with NETWORK MARKETING, which emphasizes the direct person-to-person approach. Often time's companies which emphasize the term will have a more direct RETAIL model or person-to-person direct selling model which minimizes the emphasis on recruiting fellow DISTRIBUTORS or building a SALES ORGANIZATION. See also DIRECT SELLING, NETWORK MARKETING, and MULTI-LEVEL MARKETING.

DIRECT SELLING- term refers to the emphasis on DIRECT SALES, and selling directly person-to-person. See also DIRECT SALES.

DIRECT SELLING ASSOCIATION (DSA)- according to www.dsa.org , "The Direct Selling Association (DSA) is the national trade association of the leading firms that manufacture and distribute goods and services sold directly to consumers. Approximately 200 companies are members of the association, including many well-known brand names." For a NETWORK COMPANY to be a member of the DSA they are required to apply, uniform their POLICIES AND PROCEDURES with DSA regulations, and pay a significant (recurring) fee. In return these companies are allowed to claim themselves as part of this association. Being a member of the DSA is not a requirement for NETWORK MARKETING COMPANIES, and does not guarantee any protection, and is not a statement of the ethics of a NETWORK MARKETING COMPANY or quality of a PRODUCT.

DISCOUNTED VOLUME- (1) a term that indicates that the amount of PRODUCT VOLUME, QUALIFYING VOLUME, or COMMISSIONABLE VOLUME has been discounted in relation to the amount of SALES VOLUME or compared to the SALES PRICE of the PRODUCT that was sold or distributed. DISCOUNTED VOLUME can be a standard notion within a COMPANY where all or most products carry with them a lower amount of PV, QV, or CV than the SALE PRICE of the PRODUCT. This can be used to either help the PRODUCT be priced within a reasonable market, or it can be a tool of manipulation to maximize profits while minimizing COMMISSIONS. (2) There are also circumstances where the respective VOLUME levels may be discounted temporarily on an ORDER as a result of actions utilized within a COMPENSATION PLAN. As an order may qualify for generating a particular COMMISSION, VOLUME from that order may be discounted in relation to other COMMISSIONS or RANK QUALIFICATIONS. This is usually completed to fund COMMISSIONS in a priority rating, where one BONUS may be given higher priority than another BONUS, while attempting to maintain the budgeted cost of the COMPENSATION PLAN. Most commonly this type of DISCOUNTED VOLUME happens in relation to high COMMISSIONS generated on FAST START VOLUME, to avoid an over payment of COMMISSION on a PRODUCT when paid in conjunction with other BONUSES.

DISTRIBUTOR- an abbreviated or casual term for an INDEPENDENT DISTRIBUTOR (ID), INDEPENDENT BUSINESS OWNER (IBO), INDEPENDENT PRODUCT CONSULTANT (IPC), WHOLESALE DISTRIBUTOR, and ASSOCIATE. This term identifies the individual as a WHOLESALE purchaser, a retailer, a distributor, recruiter, or someone who has the potential to do so in conjunction with a previously agreed to arraignment (DISTRIBUTOR AGREEMENT AND APPLICATION). It is also the general term for the highest involved CUSTOMER TYPE within any NETWORK MARKETING COMPANY. Refer to INDEPENDENT DISTRIBUTOR (ID) for full definition. See also CUSTOMER and PREFERRED CUSTOMER.

DISTRIBUTOR APPLICATION (OR AGREEMENT)- a required document to be collected or electronically completed and agreed to which collects DISTRIBUTOR Data and presents a binding agreement between the applying DISTRIBUTOR and the NETWORK MARKETING COMPANY. The data collected on the application usually consists of the following for the primary and secondary applicants: date of application, name, business names, social security information or government tax identification number, contact information, COMMISSION payment method, DIRECT DEPOSIT information, initial ORDER, optional AUTOSHIP ORDER, credit card information, and applicant's signature and agreement to the terms of the application. The terms of the DISTRIBUTOR APPLICATION OR AGREEMENT traditionally relate specifically to accepting and abiding by the published POLICIES AND PROCEDURES (usually not directly presented on the application), the automatic charge of the payment method provided, and any other legal terms presented with the application. The DISTRIBUTOR APPLICATION OR AGREEMENT when executed becomes a binding document as part of the COMPANIES POLICIES AND PROCEDURES.

DISTRIBUTOR NETWORK SERVICES (DNS)- a department within the NETWORK MARKETING'S corporate structure that manages the direct services for the INDEPENDENT DISTRIBUTOR force for the COMPANY. This often is an umbrella term which includes many smaller departments such as CUSTOMER SERVICE, ORDER ENTRY, LEADERSHIP or ELITE SERVICES, and virtual service requests. This term can also be synonymous with: CUSTOMER SERVICE, ORDER ENTRY DEPARTMENT, and CALL CENTER. See also SALES DEPARTMENT and MARKETING DEPARTMENT.

DOWNLINE- refers to an individual or group of individuals who are within the SALES TEAM or ORGANIZATION of another INDEPENDENT DISTRIBUTOR, either through a GENEALOGY of SPONSORING or PLACEMENT within their TEAM or ORGANIZATION. This term refers to distributors or customers that an INDEPENDENT DISTRIBUTOR has the opportunity to benefit from within the ORGANIZATION. See also UPLINE.

DUPLICATION- term used in NETWORK MARKETING that indicates the degree in which a TEAM or DISTRIBUTOR'S activity in relation to ENROLLING, training, and SPONSORING has been trained and duplicated by other members or TEAMS within the DISTRIBUTOR'S

ORGANIZATION. DUPLICATION is the key to successful NETWORK MARKETING, and is therefore the desire of every network marketer. ENROLLING can generate revenue and COMMISSIONS, but DUPLICATION magnifies EARNINGS significantly. A common phrase in relation to DUPLICATION in NETWORK MARKETING is, "A networker would rather have 1% effort from 100 people than 100% effort from 1."

DYNAMIC COMPRESSION (COMPRESSED)- type of COMPRESSION which is intended to minimize BREAKAGE within the COMPENSATION PLAN. COMPRESSED DYNAMIC COMPRESSION is usually termed DYNAMIC COMPRESSION, and is often confused with the ORIGINAL DYNAMIC COMPRESSION which is also often usually termed in literature as DYNAMIC COMPRESSION. COMPRESSED DYNAMIC COMPRESSION is an attempted enhancement to the ORIGINAL DYNAMIC COMPRESSION - please review definition for DYNAMIC COMPRESSION (ORIGINAL). In COMPRESSED DYNAMIC COMPRESSION, as the COMMISSIONS or order moves up the TREE, and finds the next DISTRIBUTOR who qualifies to be paid on that transaction (or EARNINGS), if that DISTRIBUTOR qualifies for a LEVEL of COMMISSIONS that exceeds that level that the COMMISSION ENGINE is looking to pay, than those subsequent levels and all in between what the engine is looking for and what the DISTRIBUTOR qualifies for compresses and is paid to that DISTRIBUTOR. This allows DISTRIBUTORS to earn and qualify for multiple LEVELS of COMMISSIONS and payout on the same DISTRIBUTOR, ORDER, or EARNINGS. A result of this COMPRESSION minimizes BREAKAGE, but also minimizes leader payout in the long run, as ORGANIZATIONS evolve, and TEAM members begin to qualify to higher RANKS essentially capturing COMMISSIONS that normally would have rolled up the TREE. In COMPRESSED DYNAMIC COMPRESSION the DISTRIBUTORS have the potential to earn more on their individual TEAM members, but eventually earn on fewer TEAM members in the long run. COMPRESSED DYNAMIC COMPRESSION is a classic example in the INDUSTRY of a failed attempted to enhance an already unique, stable, and profitable concept. See also COMPRESSION, DYNAMIC COMPRESSION (ORIGINAL), and STANDARD COMPRESSION.

DYNAMIC COMPRESSION (ORIGINAL)- type of COMPRESSION which is intended to minimize BREAKAGE within the COMPENSATION PLAN. ORIGINAL DYNAMIC COMPRESSION is usually termed DYNAMIC COMPRESSION, and can be confused with the COMPRESSED DYNAMIC COMPRESSION which is also often usually termed in literature as DYNAMIC COMPRESSION. DYNAMIC COMPRESSION (ORIGINAL) looks from the order and pays up the tree a number of times. If there are nine LEVELS that could be paid out in the COMPENSATION PLAN, then each order tries to pay out nine times up the tree to nine separate individuals or positions. The COMMISSION ENGINE takes the order and looks up to see who qualifies for the first LEVEL (or in other words who qualified to have it paid out the first time). After it is paid out the first time (or LEVEL), it looks further up the tree for a second LEVEL, and then a third, and so on (based on RANK QUALIFICATIONS). In this process, if it is paid out five times and needs to skip twenty people to find the next person who qualified for a sixth LEVEL, it does so. This type of DYNAMIC COMPRESSION maximizes the payout of the leaders, while minimizing the BREAKAGE to the COMPANY. If the plan has fixed percentage payouts, this type of COMPRESSION does not eliminate BREAKAGE; it only minimizes the BREAKAGE, but does a very good job of it. In COMPENSATION PLANS that may have a FLUCTUATING PERCENTAGE based on BREAKAGE, this type of COMPRESSION can entirely eliminate BREAKAGE. Either way, this type of COMPRESSION yields the most fair and balanced CHECKS for the leaders, and helps them fairly reach deep into their ORGANIZATION, and is therefore, the most sought after. See also DYNAMIC COMPRESSION (COMPRESSED), COMPRESSION, and STANDARD COMPRESSION.

E

EARNING POTENTIAL- a marketable phrase that indicates the most an INDEPENDENT DISTRIBUTOR may earn either from a particular BONUS or from the COMPENSATION PLAN as a whole. Term is intended to look less like an income CAP, which can carry with it a negative connotation. Often times EARNING POTENTIALS are enforced using direct CAPS, but can also just refer to the potential earnings that can be distributed to the DISTRIBUTOR through the COMPENSATION PLAN (often still considered to be the most possible an DISTRIBUTOR can earn). Term can often be synonymous with CAPS and POTENTIAL.

EARNINGS- refers to the monetary payments of COMMISSIONS earned by an INDEPENDENT DISTRIBUTOR through a NETWORK MARKETING COMPANY. EARNINGS may include multiple COMMISSIONS and BONUSES, and in most circumstances are taxable by law and included in the issued 1099 yearly. See also COMMISSIONS and COMMISSION PAYMENTS.

ELITE SERVICES- an extension of DISTRIBUTOR NETWORK SERVICES or the CALL CENTER intended to have committed representatives dedicated to the leading DISTRIBUTOR force. In most companies, when a DISTRIBUTOR reaches a pre-determined LEADERSHIP RANK, they are allowed to have direct access to a personal representative (who may also be handling other leading DISTRIBUTOR accounts) that is able to be their direct contact for corporate support and information. Term is synonymous with LEADERSHIP SERVICES. See also DISTRIBUTOR NETWORK SERVICES, MARKETING DEPARTMENT, and SALE DEPARTMENT.

ENROLLEE- term refers to the DISTRIBUTOR or CUSTOMER that is being or has been ENROLLED into the NETWORK MARKETING COMPANY or TEAM ORGANIZATION. This term is strongly connected with being SPONSORED. See also ENROLLER.

ENROLLER- the parent DISTRIBUTOR whom is or has personally introduced and ENROLLED the CHILD or DOWNLINE DISTRIBUTOR into the ORGANIZATION. Term can be synonymous with SPONSOR. See also PARENT.

ENROLLING- refers to the act of joining a NETWORK MARKETING COMPANY as an INDEPENDENT DISTRIBUTOR, or in SPONSORING someone into a NETWORK MARKETING COMPANY. ENROLLING requires an application to be completed and any subsequent documents to be agreed to. See also DISTRIBUTOR AGREEMENT and SPONSOR.

ENROLLMENT BONUS- refers to a BONUS within the COMPENSATION PLAN or COMMISSION engine which pays on the SALES from recently enrolled DISTRIBUTORS. These BONUSES are usually short term BONUSES with a higher COMMISSION rate to the direct SPONSOR, and can also be referred to as FAST START BONUSES. ENROLLMENT bonuses can also be confused with a RECRUITING BONUS, or RECRUITING BONUSES can be marketed as ENROLLMENT BONUSES. See FAST START BONUS for a more complete definition.

ENROLLMENT TREE- TREE which details the ENROLLING or SPONSORING activity of an INDEPENDENT DISTRIBUTOR and the DISTRIBUTORS within his personal ENROLLMENT TREE ORGANIZATION. ENROLLMENT TREES are usually always UNILEVEL TREES in that it detailed the genealogy of ENROLLMENT activity, and therefore can contain multiple LEGS, and unlimited LEVELS. The first level of the ENROLLMENT TREE will detail those who are directly enrolled by the INDEPENDENT DISTRIBUTOR regardless of placement within any other TREE structure supported by the NETWORK MARKETING COMPANY. As those individuals on the first LEVEL of the ENROLLMENT TREE begin enrolling other DISTRIBUTORS themselves (their own first LEVEL), those new ENROLLMENTS are detailed as the second LEVEL of the original INDEPENDENT DISTRIBUTOR. There are many BONUSES and RANK requirements or QUALIFICATIONS which may be calculated or determined by the ENROLLMENT TREE. Often times this is called the hidden TREE within many COMPANIES, as it is built in the background of the COMPANY and is build regardless of intent. Term can be synonymous with SPONSOR TREE. See also UNILEVEL TREE, BINARY TREE, MATRIX TREE, and TREE.

ENROLLMENT TREE VOLUME- the amount of total PRODUCT VOLUME accumulated throughout the entire ENROLLMENT TREE ORGANIZATION within a given COMMISSION or QUALIFICATION PERIOD. This VOLUME sums the VOLUME within all ENROLLMENT TREE LEGS. This can also refer to ORGANIZATION VOLUME within the respective ENROLLMENT TREE STRUCTURE.

EVENT- a scheduled meeting, PARTY, or CONVENTION with the intention of MARKETING, sharing, or education on a COMPANY'S PRODUCT, COMPENSATION PLAN, OPPORTUNITY, or NETWORK MARKETING as a whole. Examples of EVENTS related to NETWORK MARKETING: CONVENTION, OPPORTUNITY MEETING, PARTY, PRODUCT MEETING (TRAINING), and REGIONAL EVENT.

EWALLET- a method of being paid or paying COMMISSIONS or EARNINGS from a NETWORK MARKETING COMPANY through an electronic wallet or online account. Often these electronic wallets are accessible via the internet and allow the INDEPENDENT DISTRIBUTOR to then transfer their EARNINGS into a bank account, convert into a different currency, or collect for a future transaction period. EWALLETS are most often used as a method of funding commissions earned through the compensation plan to international markets (particularly countries still under an NFR PROGRAM) where EARNINGS are funded in one currency, but need to be converted into another currency before deposit is initiated into a local bank account. Recently, EWALLET have become more common for domestic markets, as it allows for additional tools and resources to be offered to the INDEPENDENT DISTRIBUTOR. See also CHECK, PAY CARD, and DIRECT DEPOSIT.

EXECUTIVE- top corporate team member of the NETWORK MARKETING COMPANY within the CORPORATE ENVIRONMENT. These include all the Chief Officers, and usually some, if not all of the Vice Presidents.

F

FAST START BONUS- a temporary BONUS that is offered or earned upon the ENROLLMENT of a new DISTRIBUTOR. Often times can be synonymous with ENROLLMENT BONUS. This can also refer to BONUSES that are only offered for a short period of time for the newly enrolled DISTRIBUTOR. These BONUSES can also be referred to by the slang term as RECRUITING BONUSES, because they pay as a result of the purchases made by newly enrolled DISTRIBUTORS. FAST START BONUSES pay on the activity of a newly enrolled DISTRIBUTOR, and are usually higher paying BONUSES, with the intention of financially incentivizing the action of enrolling new DISTRIBUTORS and increasing their initial purchases. It is statistically true, that most DISTRIBUTORS pay more in their first orders than at any other time in the DISTRIBUTOR life cycle. FAST START BONUSES are one aspect of the three generic REQUIREMENTS of a NETWORK MARKETING COMPENSATION PLAN; other generic REQUIREMENTS would be RESIDUAL BONUSES (OR COMMISSIONS) and LEADERSHIP BONUSES.

FAST START VOLUME- refers to volume that is purchased by a DISTRIBUTOR who has a FAST START or ENROLLMENT BONUS paid on their ORDERS to their SPONSOR. Often times this indicates that this VOLUME will be discounted for other BONUSES as long as the order is being COMMISSIONED for a FAST START or ENROLLMENT BONUS. This is also any VOLUME which is used in the calculation of a specific FAST START BONUS or ENROLLMENT BONUS.

FIELD- refers to the DISTRIBUTOR force or population that is selling or distributing the PRODUCT, SERVICE, or OPPORTUNITY as a whole. Term is usually used to describe all DISTRIBUTORS or AFFILIATES of a COMPANY that are not officially associated with the CORPORATE ENVIRONMENT.

FLUSHED VOLUME- refers to VOLUME that may have once been available to a DISTRIBUTOR but for one reason or another is flushed or lost, usually as a result of an inactive status within the COMPENSATION PLAN or POLICIES AND PROCEDURES of the COMPANY. Universally, this term refers to any VOLUME that is used or lost, and therefore is no longer available for the purpose of QUALIFICATIONS or COMMISSIONS. When VOLUME is flushed, the VOLUME will never be made available again. Many BINARY ORGANIZATIONS emphasize the importance of CARRY OVER VOLUME in the COMPENSATION PLAN, yet they all have parameters around how, where, when, and why any remaining or CARRY OVER VOLUME will flush or be removed. See also CARRY OVER VOLUME.

FORCED MATRIX- a type of MATRIX TREE STRUCTURE that automatically forces placement of newly ENROLLED DISTRIBUTORS in an attempt to fill out the MATRIX ORGANIZATION. In a FORCED MATRIX each level is required to be filled before the SPONSORING DISTRIBUTOR can being to place on the subsequent LEVELS of their ORGANIZATION. Also see MATRIX (STRUCTURE) for a complete definition.

FOUNDER- title which indicates that the individual is an original creator, investor, or FOUNDER of the NETWORK MARKETING COMPANY.

G

Genealogy- often times refers to the organization TREE or STRUCTURE. GENEALOGY details the ENROLLING or SPONSORING activities of an individual and the SPONSORING activities of the other members within the GENEALOGY or ORGANIZATION TREE. Term can also be used generically to refer to the PLACEMENT, or PLACEMENT TREE, of an ORGANIZATION. GENEALOGY usually is directly connected to any structure detailing the relationships within the ORGANIZATION, which would be beneficial to track for either QUALIFICATIONS or COMMISSIONS.

Generation- is defined as the members within the GENEALOGY TREE or ORGANIZATION STRUCTURE that are positioned between two higher ranking members of the ORGANIZATION. Usually, all GENERATION defining RANKS are determined by an intermediate RANK that is similar or equal to the RANK that begins to qualify to earn said GENERATION benefits or BONUS payout. GENERATIONS are often, but not always, determined from QUALIFICATION PERIOD to QUALIFICATION PERIOD, and therefore, the size and value of a GENERATION can regularly change and adjust according to the QUALIFICATIONS of other members within the ORGANIZATION. A prime example within COMPENSATION PLANS, would be similar to the following quotation, "A GENERATION is defined from one RANK 5 or above, down to and including the next RANK 5 or above within the ORGANIZATION." GENERATIONS are usually determined through following all LEGS to determining RANK QUALIFIED generational breaks. GENERATIONS can define the value of additional BONUSES, matching programs, or QUALIFICATION requirements. Some GENERATIONS will include the DISTRIBUTOR that ends the GENERATION (particularly in matching programs), and some may not.

GENERATIONS (PROGRESSIVE)- a more uncommon way to view DYNAMIC COMPRESSION (ORIGINAL). In PROGRESSIVE GENERATIONS each GENERATION requires a higher RANK than the previous GENERATION to define the end of each subsequent GENERATION. The end result is the size of each subsequent GENERATION grows larger and larger. Another end result is that the highest ranking member of the ORGANIZATION usually will always maximize or capture on everyone within the ORGANIZATION. A prime example of this type of PROGRESSIVE GENERATIONS would be the following: A DISTRIBUTOR'S first GENERATION is determined from them down to and including the next RANK 5 or above within the ORGANIZATION; the second generation will start where the first GENERATION ends down to and including the next RANK 6 or above; the third from the end of the second to the next RANK 7 or above, etc. The potential result of PROGRESSIVE GENERATIONS is that each PROGRESSIVE GENERATION may include the equivalent of multiple standard GENERATIONS. A more common view of this concept is seen as the ORIGINAL DYNAMIC COMPRESSION. Although it is explained differently, DYNAMIC COMPRESSION (from the bottom up) and PROGRESSIVE GENERATIONS (from the top down) the end result is usually exactly the same.

GENERATION VOLUME- the total accumulated VOLUME during a COMMISSION or QUALIFICATION PERIOD within a defined GENERATION for the PERIOD.

GROUP VOLUME (GV)- the total accumulated VOLUME during a COMMISSION or QUALIFICATION PERIOD within a particular GROUP or ORGANIZATION. GROUP VOLUME can either refer to an entire GROUP or ORGANIZATION, or a part of an ORGANIZATION that has been defined as an individual group for the purposes of COMMISSIONS or QUALIFICATIONS.

HYBRID BINARY- a COMPENSATION PLAN that allows two separate STRUCTURE TYPES (or TREES) to be built in order to allow different BONUSES to be calculated. The most common HYBRID BINARY attempts to combine a BINARY structure and a UNILEVEL structure, allowing both TREES to be built at the same time and to offer different BONUSES to flow through the separate TREES. HYBRID BINARIES usually place the BINARY in the forefront of all their marketing literature emphasizing the unity, retention, and growth that takes place in most BINARIES, while having the UNILEVEL structure maintained for higher BONUSES to allow for larger COMMISSIONS for leaders within the ORGANIZATION. HYBRID BINARIES can have a wide range of BONUSES based on both TREES. See also UNILEVEL, CYCLE BINARY, and WEAK LEG BINARY.

I

INACTIVE (FOR BONUSES)- term indicating that the DISTRIBUTOR account is not currently ACTIVE (FOR BONUSES) or personally QUALIFIED for earning a particular BONUS or all BONUSES presented within a NETWORK MARKETING COMPANIES COMPENSATION or COMMISSION PLAN. This indicates that a minimal QUALIFICATION has not been met by the DISTRIBUTOR to qualify for any BONUSES; usually this refers to a lack of accumulated PERSONAL VOLUME most commonly from not placing a personal ORDER or accumulating a required amount of personal SALES for the particular QUALIFICATION PERIOD. Being INACTIVE (FOR BONUSES) does not reflect and is not directly correlated with being INACTIVE (FOR ORDERING). See also ACTIVE (FOR BONUSES), BONUSES, COMPENSATION PLAN, and QUALIFICATIONS.

INACTIVE (FOR ORDERING)- term indicating that the DISTRIBUTOR account is no longer allowed to place orders, or participate in the COMPANY'S offerings until the account is restored to ACTIVE (FOR ORDERING) status. A DISTRIBUTOR'S account can be deemed INACTIVE (FOR ORDERING) by not following the guidelines in the POLICIES AND PROCEDURES for remaining ACTIVE (FOR ORDERING), as a result of being Suspended pending an investigation by the Compliance Department, or the account being Terminated.

Incentives- commission bonuses, promotions, or recognition towards encouraging a type of activity or behavior within the sales organization. See also Compensation Plan, Bonuses, and Leadership.

Independent Business Owner (IBO)- a term used by some network marketing companies for an Independent Distributor. These companies use this term in an effort to emphasis the business opportunity of a Distributor owning their own business, and the legitimacy of the compensation plan. Refer to Independent Distributor for full definition; also synonymous with Independent Product Consultant (IPC), Wholesale Distributor, and Associate. See also Distributor.

Independent Distributor (ID)- a customer type of a network marketing company which denotes the privilege to distribute the product or service of the company; may also be referred to simply as a Distributor. After having agreed to a Distributor Application or Agreement, company Policies and Procedures, and paid any enrollment fees, the Independent Distributor is allowed to purchase the company's product or services at wholesale price, resell at retail, enroll other distributors, and participate in the company's compensation plan. Independent Distributors are not direct representatives of the company but are only wholesale distributors encouraged and incentivized (through the compensation plan) to generate sales for the company and for their own compensation. The term 'Independent' denotes that the distributor's statements, claims, and marketing actions in

43

regards to financial results or product efficacy are only repre-
sentations of the DISTRIBUTOR themselves, and not statements or
claims which the COMPANY is held primarily liable for (unless
such actions are known, encouraged, or solicited by the
COMPANY). INDEPENDENT DISTRIBUTORS are only deemed as such, so
as long as they remain ACTIVE (FOR ORDERING) by being in good
standing with the company's POLICIES AND PROCEDURES and are up
to date on any fees associated with being an INDEPENDENT
DISTRIBUTOR. The term INDEPENDENT DISTRIBUTOR is synonymous
with the following terms throughout the industry (many companies use different terms to describe the same CUSTOMER TYPE):
INDEPENDENT BUSINESS OWNER (IBO), INDEPENDENT PRODUCT
CONSULTANT (IPC), WHOLESALE DISTRIBUTOR, and ASSOCIATE. See also
DISTRIBUTOR, CUSTOMER, and PREFERRED CUSTOMER.

INDEPENDENT PRODUCT CONSULTANT (IPC)- a term used by some
NETWORK MARKETING COMPANIES for an INDEPENDENT DISTRIBUTOR.
These companies use this term in an effort to emphasis the
PRODUCT'S importance within the INDUSTRY, the roll of the
DISTRIBUTOR in sharing the PRODUCT with others, and attempts to
downplay the OPPORTUNITY or NETWORK MARKETING aspect of the
business. Refer to INDEPENDENT DISTRIBUTOR for full definition;
also synonymous with INDEPENDENT BUSINESS OWNER (IBO),
WHOLESALE DISTRIBUTOR, and ASSOCIATE. See also DISTRIBUTOR.

INDIRECT PRODUCT- an intangible PRODUCT that may be offered by
the COMPANY directly or indirectly within the MARKETING literature. Examples of INDIRECT PRODUCTS may include things such as
personal development, personal fulfillment, culture, growth
opportunity, financial security, the COMPENSATION PLAN, timing
within NETWORK MARKETING, or other concepts that are not direct-

ly sold within the sales transaction. INDIRECT PRODUCTS can either be directly marketed as part of the offering, or as a innate consequence of the offering. See also PRODUCT.

INDUSTRY, THE – slang term used to describe the whole of the NETWORK MARKETING INDUSTRY, including all NETWORK MARKETING, DIRECT SALES, and COMMISSION based COMPANIES and their traits, trends, and practices. This term refers to behavior and activity as a whole (including CORPORATE ENVIRONMENTS and FIELD behaviors).

INDUSTRY STANDARDS- terms that are commonly used or have been accepted as standard terms within an industry. In NETWORK MARKETING, INDUSTRY STANDARDS are very minimally accepted from COMPANY to COMPANY, as many COMPANIES are able to manipulate MARKETING literature and alter the realistic impression of the COMPANY, PRODUCT, or COMPENSATION PLAN. Often times each COMPANY will use common terms, and redefine what that term means as a result of a lack of accepted or enforced INDUSTRY STANDARD terms or definitions. There is a great need for increased and defined INDUSTRY STANDARDS within the world on NETWORK MARKETING.

INSIDE LEG- Refers to the UNCOMMON LEG, or the LEG OPPOSITE to the OUTSIDE or COMMON LEG. Term is usually used in relation to BINARY ORGANIZATIONS, indicating the portion of the ORGANIZATION that is not in the direct line of commonly shared support in ORGANIZATION growth. By nature all BINARIES have at least one INSIDE LEG or UNCOMMON LEG, that falls directly on the responsibility of the INDEPENDENT DISTRIBUTOR to build with little or no direct support.

K

KIT- refers to a collection of PRODUCTS or an introduction packet ordered and sent to a DISTRIBUTOR upon ENROLLMENT.

L

LEADER- refers to a top RANKING, ENROLLING, or most active DISTRIBUTORS within an ORGANIZATION or NETWORK MARKETING COMPANY. See also LEADERSHIP.

LEADERSHIP- can refer to a quality that a LEADER within an ORGANIZATION posses, or to the collection of qualities within an ORGANIZATION as a whole. This term can also refer to a population of people or LEADERS within an ORGANIZATION. These usually are related or classified by the top RANKS within the ORGANIZATION. Effective LEADERSHIP within an ORGANIZATION is the key to building a successful TEAM. LEADERSHIP often is denoted by the quality of the activity within the DOWNLINE of an

ORGANIZATION, as well as the DUPLICATION which takes place within a TEAM.

LEADERSHIP BONUS- BONUSES or COMMISSION POOLS that are allocated to be distributed to the higher ranking DISTRIBUTORS within a NETWORK MARKETING COMPANY. These POOLS usually contain a percentage of the TOTAL COMPANY COMMISSIONABLE VOLUME that is accumulated and then distributed to the top leaders through the defined BONUS requirements within a NETWORK MARKETING COMPANY'S published COMPENSATION PLAN literature. LEADERS BONUSES are created to incentivize leadership, to reward leading behavior, and to retain key leaders within an ORGANIZATION. LEADERSHIP BONUSES are one aspect of the three generic requirements of a NETWORK MARKETING COMPENSATION PLAN; other generic REQUIREMENTS would be RESIDUAL BONUSES (OR COMMISSIONS) and FAST START BONUSES.

LEADERSHIP SERVICES- an extension of DISTRIBUTOR NETWORK SERVICES or the CALL CENTER intended to have committed representatives dedicated to the leading DISTRIBUTOR force. In most companies, when a DISTRIBUTOR reaches a pre-determined RANK, they are allowed to have direct access to a personal representative (who may also be handling other leading DISTRIBUTOR accounts) that is able to be their direct contact for corporate support and information. Term is synonymous with ELITE SERVICES. See also DISTRIBUTOR NETWORK SERVICES, MARKETING DEPARTMENT, and SALE DEPARTMENT.

LEAD GENERATORS- programs in which DISTRIBUTORS can purchase or acquire a population of LEADS. These programs usually collect data from numerous sources, including internet affiliate groups and capture pages, and can include people who have shown some interest in something related with the COMPANY (e.g. earning additional income, the PRODUCT, health, nutrition, etc.). LEAD GENERATORS only capture information that can be passed or sold to another individual who will then attempt to contact and make the sale or generate a new ENROLLMENT for their ORGANIZATION.

LEADS- individuals who are currently not a CUSTOMER or DISTRIBUTOR of the NETWORK MARKETING COMPANY, who are potentially future CUSTOMERS or DISTRIBUTORS.

LEFT LEG (BINARY)- refers to the LEFT LEG or team in the BINARY ORGANIZATION. LEFT LEGS are to the left side of the ORGANIZATION as the DISTRIBUTOR is looking at the ORGANIZATION, not as if they are inside or looking down upon the ORGANIZATION. See also RIGHT LEG.

LEFT LEG (MATRIX)- refers to the LEFT LEG in the MATRIX ORGANIZATION. LEFT LEGS are to the left side of the ORGANIZATION as the DISTRIBUTOR is looking at the ORGANIZATION, not as if they are inside or looking down the ORGANIZATION. See also RIGHT LEG (MATRIX) and CENTER LEG (MATRIX).

LEG RANK- the highest paid RANK of an INDEPENDENT DISTRIBUTOR within that LEG of the ORGANIZATION for the given COMMISSION or QUALIFICATION PERIOD.

LEGS- refer to the amount of personally placed or enrolled DISTRIBUTORS to another DISTRIBUTOR. Each personally connected DISTRIBUTOR to another DISTRIBUTOR is classified as the beginning of a LEG within the ORGANIZATION. Every direct connection or connected branch of the ORGANIZATION to the INDEPENDENT DISTRIBUTOR is a LEG. BINARY ORGANIZATIONS by nature have two LEGS and UNILEVEL ORGANIZATIONS are not limited in the amount of personal connections or LEG that can be built. More specific terms related to the types of LEGS within an ORGANIZATION may be any of the following: BINARY LEG, CENTER LEG (MATRIX), COMMON LEG, INSIDE LEG, LEFT LEG, LESSER LEG, OUTSIDE LEG, PAY LEG, POWER LEG, RIGHT LEG, STRONG LEG, UNCOMMON LEG, UNILEVEL LEG, WEAK LEG.

LEG VOLUME- the total amount of accumulated VOLUME within a particular LEG in an organization for a COMMISSION or QUALIFICATION PERIOD.

LESSER LEG- a term used in BINARY structures (usually WEAK LEG BINARIES) to describe the LEG that contains the least amount of VOLUME between the two LEGS of the BINARY ORGANIZATION. Term is synonymous with PAY LEG and WEAKER LEG. LESSER LEGS are often used in the qualification requirements of the published COMPENSATION PLAN, and at times can be directly connected to the potential COMMISSIONS earned. See also STRONG LEG.

LEVEL- each tier within the GENEALOGY. Those personally connected to the DISTRIBUTOR would be considered their first LEVEL, and those connected to them would be considered the DISTRIBUTORS second LEVEL. In NETWORK MARKETING the DISTRIBUTOR creates LEVELS within their organization through the ENROLLMENT and DUPLICATION of their TEAM. LEVELS can also be a way to determine the separation, through ENROLLMENT or PLACEMENT within an ORGANIZATION TREE, between one DISTRIBUTOR and another.

LIMITS- limitations, barriers or boundaries. These can define the LIMITS with the EARNING POTENTIAL of a DISTRIBUTOR within a COMPENSATION PLAN, or the limitation in building an ORGANIZATION. This is a general term to describe the barriers within any COMPANY, activity, or behavior. Also see CAP for more details.

LINEAR (STRUCTURE)- any TREE structure supported by the NETWORK MARKETING COMPANY which builds the ORGANIZATION horizontally instead of vertically. Very uncommon within the INDUSTRY, and with as many variations as there are LINEAR plans (currently no two LINEAR plans are alike), a LINEAR building structure doesn't' follow the conventional building techniques or COMMISSION BONUS methods of the more traditional UNILEVEL, BINARY, or MATRIX. Usually what defines LINEAR plans are as ORGANIZATIONS mature, instead of developing deeper ORGANIZATION pay is determined by the behavior of building wider, more complex ORGANIZATIONS.

LINES- another term for LEG. Each LEG of an organization can also be called a LINE of the ORGANIZATION. Also see LEG for more details.

LIST, THE- See "THE LIST" for definition.

MARKETING (CORPORATE)- the actions, material, and culture that is developed and built by the CORPORATE ENVIRONMENT to generate a brand image of a PRODUCT or COMPANY. CORPORATE MARKETING is indented to create the look, feel, story, culture, price, and positioning of a PRODUCT. All CORPORATE MARKETING is required to be generic and support a common story or theme in order to allow or accommodate universal actions of multiple INDEPENDENT DISTRIBUTORS. CORPORATE MARKETING is often confused with DISTRIBUTOR MARKETING. Where DISTRIBUTOR MARKETING is designed to make the DIRECT SALE, CORPORATE MARKETING is only to facilitate to the DISTRIBUTOR the freedom to use the created brand, image, and position to help aid in their respective and independent activates to generate SALES. CORPORATE MARKETING minimizes claims or the DIRECT SALES push in an effort to limit liabilities to the COMPANY and the DISTRIBUTOR FIELD as a whole. See also MARKETING (DISTRIBUTOR).

MARKETING (DISTRIBUTOR)- the actions, material, or sales practices that is done independent of the CORPORATE staff by the DISTRIBUTOR FIELD in an effort to generate or increase SALES. Often times literature or MARKETING activity by the DISTRIBUTOR is more directed or specific to the MARKETING or position that a particular INDEPENDENT DISTRIBUTOR has decided to focus on. DISTRIBUTOR MARKETING is traditionally much more liberal, and although should still be accountable legally to the CORPORATE COMPANY, it is much more focused on the actual SALE of the product, or the close. CORPORATE MARKETING and DISTRIBUTOR MARKETING rarely mixes, nor should it; if there are circumstances where CORPORATE MARKETING mixes with the DISTRIBUTOR MARKETING it usually increases liability and decreases universally DISTRIBUTOR options or freedom to market. See also MARKETING (CORPORATE).

MARKETING DEPARTMENT- department within a NETWORK MARKETING COMPANY CORPORATE ENVIRONMENT which manages and executes the corporate MARKETING direction. This department handles corporate issue literature, videos, product positioning, industry pricing, labeling, and many other corporate MARKETING endeavors including but not limited to the look, feel, experience, and presence of the COMPANY. See also MARKETING (CORPORATE).

MATCHING BONUS- refers to a BONUS or COMMISSION in the COMPENSATION PLAN where one DISTRIBUTOR is able to match a percentage of the earnings of another DISTRIBUTOR within his ORGANIZATION. MATCHING BONUSES are designed to do two things within the DISTRIBUTOR field: (1) to create an incentive for DISTRIBUTORS to help other DISTRIBUTORS increase their EARNINGS, and in return increase the amount of EARNINGS that they are matching on, increasing their own check as a whole; (2) to increase COMPENSATION to the DISTRIBUTOR FIELD, by decreasing BREAKAGE, and therefore subsequently increase marketability. Most commonly, MATCHING BONUSES are seen at the tail end of COMPENSATION PLANS for the intent to maximizing mid-level and high-level leader EARNINGS. This is also because traditionally MATCHING BONUSES are more effective at the tail end where the DISTRIBUTOR has the adequate ORGANIZATION to match on and make it a meaningful and financially motivating BONUS; newer DISTRIBUTORS usually do not have the organization that would make the MATCHING BONUSES at all lucrative or behavior incentivizing. An example of this BONUS would be seen as: DISTRIBUTOR "X" qualified to match 15% of the earnings of DISTRIBUTOR "Y" in his DOWNLINE who earned $100; this would mean that DISTRIBUTOR "X" would get an additional $15 in the COMPENSATION PLAN. The power within the MATCHING BONUS is not seen within the percentage that the COMPANY matches but the population size and depth the matching is able to reach in the ORGANIZATION. In many instances these can be referred to as RESIDUAL BONUSES, but are more accurately portrayed as LEADERSHIP BONUSES.

MATRIX (BUILDING TECHNIQUE)- a common concept among inexperienced NETWORK MARKETERS that can be applied to all STRUCTURE TYPES (UNILEVEL, BINARY, and MATRIX). As a building technique, building in a MATRIX fashion means that the PLACEMENT of new INDEPENDENT DISTRIBUTORS are inserted within the closest or next available position regardless of other considerations or possibilities. This action attempts to fill out the respective LEVELS within the structure entirely, while minimizing holes or empty positions for the sake of appearance. Building in a MATRIX fashion is usually not the most profitable action within the INDUSTRY, unless there are particular BONUSES associated with such an action, or the action is enforced as it is within the MATRIX (STRUCTURE).

MATRIX (STRUCTURE)- a STRUCTURE TYPE that has the highest degree of enforced structure. Within a MATRIX structure, INDEPENDENT DISTRIBUTORS are forced or required to maintain or build within a particular fashion in an effort to fill out any open positions within the TREE STRUCTURE. Different companies may require different structures within the MATRIX, but throughout the MATRIX all requirements are strictly enforced in regards to the placement of newly enrolled DISTRIBUTORS within an organization. The most common example of a MATRIX is called a "3-by-3" MATRIX where each individual is limited to only having three team legs, who are in turn only required to have three LEGS, and therefore each level increases incrementally by multiples of three. In the most common MATRIXES, there are very limited options in the form of PLACEMENT within the TREE STRUCTURE of new team members, as many of them require that the next placement go in the next or closest available position within the MATRIX. MATRIX structures traditionally are highly sought after at the beginning of new companies, and can have fast growth, but are extremely unstable once a COMPANY has began to grow; therefore, they are often not used for stable COMPANIES. Common variations within the MATRIX structures are based on the ways that the MATRIX is enforced, examples being the STANDARD MATRIX, FORCED MATRIX, and the OVER-LAID MATRIX. See also STRUCTURE TYPES, UNILEVEL, and BINARY.

MATRIX BONUS- a BONUS within the COMPENSATION PLAN which pays off of the STRUCTURE, VOLUME, or DISTRIBUTOR activity within the MATRIX TREE of an INDEPENDENT DISTRIBUTOR. This can include BONUSES which pay specific to LEG VOLUME or LEVEL VOLUME within the MATRIX TREE. All BONUSES that are paid off of the MATRIX TREE or MATRIX STRUCTURE is considered a MATRIX BONUS. These usually are considered a RESIDUAL BONUS of a COMPENSATION PLAN with a MATRIX TREE attached. Other BONUSES which pay off of the STRUCTURE TYPE of the COMPENSATION PLAN are BINARY BONUS and UNILEVEL BONUS. See also RECRUITING BONUS, FAST START BONUS, STRUCTURE BONUS, and MATCHING BONUS.

MATRIX COMMISSIONS- refers to the EARNINGS or COMMISSIONS of an INDEPENDENT DISTRIBUTOR which is earned from any MATRIX BONUSES that were QUALIFIED for and offered within the COMPENSATION PLAN. This can commonly be referred t as a RESIDUAL COMMISSION; similar to BINARY COMMISSIONS and UNILEVEL COMMISSIONS. See also COMMISSIONS, EARNINGS, and COMMISSION PAYMENTS.

MATRIX TREE- TREE which details the genealogical or PLACEMENT relationship of ENROLLMENTS or PLACEMENTS within the confines of a MATRIX structure. MATRIX TREES often only refer to the place-ment (not the ENROLLMENT) of the DISTRIBUTORS within an ORGANIZATION; and therefore classified as a PLACEMENT TREE. As with the nature of the MATRIX structure, the MATRIX TREE details a structure of a predetermined and enforced amount of LEGS within the DISTRIBUTOR'S organization. Usually, new ENROLLMENTS are placed in the closest open position within the confines of the MATRIX TREE. The main unit of consideration within the MATRIX TREE is (1) LEVEL VOLUME, (2) its relationship and compari-son with the other LEVELS of the structure, (3) and the PLACEMENT of team member in open spots in an attempt to fill the MATRIX structure to minimize open positions within the TREE. Each MATRIX TREE is only allows to as many LEGS as are predetermined by the MATRIX structure and COMPENSATION PLAN, with unlimited LEVELS of depth, but each LEVEL must be filled before personal placement can take place on the following LEVEL. MATRIX BONUSES are determined by the volume and activity within the MATRIX TREE. See also TREE, UNILEVEL TREE, ENROLLMENT TREE, SPONSOR TREE, and BINARY TREE.

MATRIX TREE VOLUME- the amount of total PRODUCT VOLUME accumulated throughout the entire MATRIX TREE STRUCTURE within a given COMMISSION or QUALIFICATION PERIOD. This VOLUME sums the VOLUME within all of the MATRIX TREE LEGS. This can also refer to ORGANIZATION VOLUME within the respective MATRIX STRUCTURE.

MONTHLY COMMISSION- EARNINGS that are QUALIFIED for within the COMPENSATION PLAN and issued MONTHLY in the form of a COMMISSION PAYMENT. Can include FAST START BONUSES, LEADERSHIP POOLS, and RESIDUAL BONUSES earned when the COMMISSION PERIOD for those BONUSES has been established by the COMPANY as a MONTHLY COMMISSION PERIOD cycle. Other COMMISSION PERIOD cycles could include WEEKLY COMMISSIONS and YEARLY COMMISSIONS depending upon what the company has deemed appropriate for their business model. Also see EARNINGS, COMMISSIONS, and BONUSES.

MULTI-LEVEL MARKETING- an older term synonymous with NETWORK MARKETING or DIRECT SALES. The term MULTI-LEVEL MARKETING emphasizes the residual potential of leveraging multi-levels of ENROLLMENT activity and the SALES efforts of multiple levels of enrolled DISTRIBUTORS. MULTI-LEVEL MARKETING is a business model used to distribute PRODUCT or SERVICES through INDEPENDENT DISTRIBUTOR who in turn is able to generate or earn COMMISSIONS for their SALES activity, and the activity within their SALES ORGANIZATION. See also NETWORK MARKETING.

N

NETWORK MARKETING- a term which can be synonymous with DIRECT SALES or MULTI-LEVEL MARKETING. The term NETWORK MARKETING emphasizes the residual potential of leveraging a network of people, or marketing through a network of direct or personal contacts. NETWORK MARKETING is a business model used to distribute PRODUCTS or SERVICES through INDEPENDENT DISTRIBUTORS who in turn are able to generate or earn COMMISSIONS for their SALES activity, and the activity within their SALES ORGANIZATION. The term NETWORK MARKETING has been the more politically correct term in recent years, as earlier companies utilizing the MULTI-LEVEL MARKETING title have not generated the most positive social image.

NETWORK MARKETING COMPANY- a specific company which utilizes the NETWORK MARKETING model.

NOT FOR RESALE (NFR)- a description or identification of an international country where the NETWORK MARKETING COMPANY is not considered to have officially opened or ON THE GROUND (OTG). The term indicates that the PRODUCT is being shipped in through customs directly to the INDEPENDENT DISTRIBUTOR and where the PRODUCT is not labeled, registered, or allowed to be retailed or resold throughout the market from the INDEPENDENT DISTRIBUTOR. NFR programs officially require that the recipient of the PRODUCT is the end PRODUCT user. Most COMPANIES will enter a country with an NFR program in an attempt to build momentum and networking growth preliminary to entering or while in the process of completing the arduous action of completing the registration of the COMPANY and PRODUCT to allow the COMPANY to be considered OTG. NFR by rule and local law carry with them very strict regulations in regard to the actions that the local INDEPENDENT DISTRIBUTOR within that market that they can take in building their business, which can include, but would not be limited to the following restictions: reselling the PRODUCT directly to others within the market, advertising, public recruiting, ordering large amounts of the PRODUCT, and having COMMISSIONS paid within the local currency. See also ON THE GROUND (OTG).

ON THE GROUND (OTG)- a description or identification of a country where the NETWORK MARKETING COMPANY is considered to be fully launched. This identification indicates that the COMPANY has a warehouse within the country, is fully registered, compliant with the local laws, and has established banking relationships to allow the purchase of PRODUCT and the COMMISSIONS to be in local currency; full COMPANY and PRODUCT registration has been completed to local and international laws. This also indicates that the INDEPENDENT DISTRIBUTORS are allows to participate fully within standard NETWORK MARKETING practices in recruiting, MARKETING, and reselling the PRODUCT within that country taking into consideration the local laws and customs. The process of opening a new market or country for a NETWORK MARKETING COMPANY as OTG is an arduous process that can take a significant amount of resources and time. This results in many NETWORK MARKETING COMPANIES to open a number of countries NFR while this registration process takes place and the infrastructure is built for the OTG program to be successful for the long run. See also NOT FOR RESALE (NFR).

OPPORTUNITY- term usually used to denote the business or profitability potential for someone within a NETWORK MARKETING COMPANY. OPPORTUNITY can therefore refer directly to the COMPENSATION PLAN or timing within the COMPANY'S life cycle, but more than likely refers potential leverage within the concept of NETWORK MARKETING as a whole. See also COMPENSATION PLAN.

OPPORTUNITY MEETING- an EVENT or scheduled meeting designed or with the intent to present to individuals or potential DISTRIBUTORS the NETWORK MARKETING COMPANY as an OPPORTUNITY to create an additional income. These meetings can often be mixed with PRODUCT MEETINGS, or PARTIES with the same intent. See also PRODUCT MEETING (TRAINING), and PARTY.

ORDER- a purchase ORDER or invoice for PRODUCT requested, paid for, sent, and delivered with the intent to acquire PRODUCT or SERVICES to consume, promote with, sell, distribute, or to fulfill any requirements established by the COMPANY'S COMPENSATION PLAN or POLICIES AND PROCEDURES. ORDERS can include those placed via phone (through the company's Representatives), over the internet, AUTOSHIP, or BUSINESS PROTECT AUTOSHIPS. ORDERS placed within a NETWORK MARKETING ORGANIZATION are usually COMMISSIONABLE; indicating that a portion of the revenue collected for the order is paid to UPLINE DISTRIBUTORS within the ORGANIZATION through the published COMPENSATION PLAN. See also BUSINESS PROTECT (AUTOSHIP) and AUTOSHIP.

ORDER ENTRY DEPARTMENT- a department within DISTRIBUTOR NETWORK SERVICES or the CALL CENTER where calls are received for the intent is to place an order with the NETWORK MARKETING COMPANY for their PRODUCT or SERVICES. Term can be synonymous with: CALL CENTER, CUSTOMER SERVICE, and DISTRIBUTOR NETWORK SERVICES.

ORGANIZATION- a term to describe a population or network of DISTRIBUTORS under a DISTRIBUTOR. The ORGANIZATION usually also denotes the team that is working or is leveraged in the COMPENSATION PLAN. ORGANIZATIONS can be identified from a number of different sources including the PLACEMENT in the TREE, LEG of the TREE, or sponsorship within the TREE. See also GENEALOGY.

OVER LAID MATRIX- a FORCED MATRIX structure where the two ORGANIZATIONS directly placed to the right and left of the DISTRIBUTOR are also forced to contribute to the DISTRIBUTOR'S team. This creates a shared MATRIX, where members of a DISTRIBUTOR'S TEAM may not just be ENROLLED by their UPLINE members, but by their sideline members, as the MATRIX ORGANIZATIONS cascade upon one another and flow into other ORGANIZATIONS. These STRUCTURES are the most unstable STRUCTURES in the

INDUSTRY, and require constant adjustment as the COMPANY and ORGANIZATION matures.

OVERRIDE- is a BONUS (or volume accumulation) where the difference between what the DOWNLINE member QUALIFIES for in the form of VOLUME or PRODUCT price discount and what the UPLINE or SPONSORING DISTRIBUTOR qualifies for rolls up to the UPLINE DISTRIBUTOR; this can relate to BONUSES, PRICING, and VOLUME. In most cases, an OVERRIDE relates directly with the cost or price level a DISTRIBUTOR qualifies for and the price level their UPLINE qualifies for. If the UPLINE qualifies for a lower price, the difference between what they qualify for and what their DOWNLINE pays for is pushed to the DISTRIBUTOR as an OVERRIDE or BONUS. In COMPENSATION PLANS which utilize OVERRIDES, there are traditionally multiple LEVELS of pricing for the same PRODUCT based on RANK. As one DISTRIBUTOR ranks higher in the ORGANIZATION, they now pay a lower price, which means they can OVERRIDE on any of their DOWNLINE who are paying a higher price and earn that difference as an OVERRIDE BONUS. These bonuses function very closely to RETAIL COMMISSIONS, but with multiple tiers and pricing options.

OVERRIDE COMPRESSION- the process by which anything non-commission based OVERRIDES, or rolls up using the same rules of an OVERRIDE bonus concept. Anything that potentially could be used (VOLUME, COMMISSIONS, RANK QUALIFICATIONS) by one DISTRIBUTOR but is not maximized, all excess, unused portions are then made available to UPLINE members who may QUALIFY for that maximization. Also see OVERRIDE.

OUTSIDE LEG- the LEG in the ORGANIZATION that is opposite from of the INSIDE LEG. Most commonly this is identified by the COMMON LEG, or the LEG that is shared with the direct UPLINE in the PLACEMENT TREE. Building the OUTSIDE LEG indicates that the DISTRIBUTOR is building that leg in a direct line with the intention of helping the growth of all of the team members within that OUTSIDE LEG of their ORGANIZATION.

P

PAID RANK- term used to describe the current RANK an INDEPENDENT DISTRIBUTOR is qualifying for and being paid at in relation to a particular COMMISSION or QUALIFICATION PERIOD from the COMPENSATION PLAN. This RANK is not necessarily associated with the PIN RANK, unless the PAID RANK is higher than the previous PIN RANK, and therefore replaces the PIN RANK as the highest RANK earned and QUALIFIED for to-date. PAID RANK directly affects the current COMMISSION CHECK, whereas PIN RANK only reflects the highest RANK QUALIFIED for RECOGNITION purposes. See also PIN RANK.

PARENT- the direct upline member or sponsor of an INDEPENDENT DISTRIBUTOR. Term is used to denote a relationship of training and mentoring within the ORGANIZATION. See also CHILD, SPONSOR, UPLINE, and DOWNLINE.

PARTY- an EVENT or scheduled meeting or PARTY usually hosted in the home of an INDEPENDENT DISTRIBUTOR with the intent to present to individuals, potential CUSTOMERS, or potential DISTRIBUTORS the PRODUCTS or OPPORTUNITY of a NETWORK MARKETING COMPANY which utilizes a PARTY PLAN strategy. PARTIES are designed to be much more of a friendlier approach, more casual, and usually emphasize on the fun culture as well as more user friendly PRODUCTS. See also PRODUCT MEETING (TRAINING) and OPPORTUNITY MEETING.

PARTY PLAN- a type of building strategy, NETWORK MARKETING COMPANY, or COMPENSATION PLAN which emphasizes the approach of holding home PARTIES with friends, neighbors, and relatives, in an effort in create SALES and generate ORGANIZATIONS.

PAY CARD- a method of being paid or paying COMMISSIONS or EARNINGS through funding a secured bank backed pre-paid credit or debit card. DISTRIBUTORS then can use the funded card to pay bills, purchase PRODUCT or other item, withdraw from, or even transfer funds into another account. These cards are usually branded by the NETWORK MARKETING COMPANY and can be used as a marketing and recruiting tool in the field as they use the card in public. PAY CARDS usually carry numerous fees and cost associated with their use, and are rarely owned or serviced by the NETWORK MARKETING COMPANY themselves but by third party vendors and support teams. In light of the most recent developments in DIRECT DEPOSIT and eWALLETS, PAY CARDS have become less popular as a stand-alone option but is often offered in conjunction with additional payment services. See also CHECK, DIRECT DEPOSIT, and eWALLET.

PAYGATE- is a BONUS (or volume accumulation) which utilizes a hybrid of the UNILEVEL TREE ORGANIZATION, the concept of GENERATIONS, and COMPRESSION. PAYGATES traditionally are paid off of a UNILEVEL TREE; and there are usually multiple PAYGATES available to be earned or qualified for from the companies that offer this program. Similar to the concept of GENERATIONS, each PAYGATE goes from the INDEPENDENT DISTRIBUTOR down to the next member of their ORGANIZATION (in each LEG) who qualifies for the same PAYGATE. The VOLUME then accumulated between the two DISTRIBUTORS is the amount that is associated with that PAYGATE for that COMMISSION or QUALIFICATION PERIOD. Often there is a VOLUME 'cost' associated with each PAYGATE, which amounts are documented in any published literature, and that cost is then deducted from the accumulated amount before the fixed percentage is then applied. Unlike GENERATIONS, each PAYGATE resets with the INDEPENDENT DISTRIBUTOR, allowing members of the organization that are in the first PAYGATE may also be associated with and contribute to all subsequent PAYGATES as well – making each PAYGATE significantly larger than the last, as each includes the member of all former PAYGATES. PAYGATES are more appropriately compared to a UNILEVEL BONUS as it pays off of the UNILEVEL TREE, and should be associated as the RESIDUAL BONUS of the compensation plan that offers this program.

PAY LEG- term is a marketable attempt in WEAK LEG BINARIES to describe the WEAK LEG; the LEG that contains the least amount of VOLUME between the TWO LEGS of the BINARY ORGANIZATION. The PAY LEG is often used in the QUALIFICATION REQUIREMENTS of the published COMPENSATION PLAN, and at times can be directly connected to the potential COMMISSIONS earned. Term is synonymous with WEAKER LEG and LESSER LEG. See also POWER LEG.

PERIOD- a pre-determined PERIOD of time in which VOLUME and requirements are accumulated for the purpose of COMMISSION payout, RANK QUALIFICATIONS, and PROMOTION BONUSES. QUALIFICATION PERIODS and COMMISSION PERIODS are examples of common PERIOD used within the INDUSTRY. PERIODS can be as long as a week, a month, or as year for some BONUSES. There can be multiple "PERIODS" within the same COMPENSATION PLAN or COMPANY, as there can be different pre-determined time frames for different BONUSES or PROMOTIONS and each can be assigned to a different span of time. The only requirement for a PERIOD is consistency and reliability.

PERSONAL VOLUME (PV)- usually a QUALIFICATION for RANK or to be ACTIVE (FOR BONUSES), and indicates the amount of PRODUCT VOLUME an INDEPENDENT DISTRIBUTOR must accumulate or has accumulated within a particular CYCLE (OF TIME) or PERIOD of time. PERSONAL VOLUME can usually be accumulated through an INDEPENDENT DISTRIBUTOR'S personal purchased ORDERS, or through the SALES of personally ENROLLED or personally retailed to CUSTOMERS (and often times PREFERRED CUSTOMERS). PERSONAL VOLUME can also directly reflect both the COMMISSIONABLE VOLUME and the QUALIFYING VOLUME the INDEPENDENT DISTRIBUTOR has accumulated for the benefit of their QUALIFICATIONS, and the QUALIFICATIONS and BONUS calculation of their UPLINE.

PIN RANK- term used to describe the highest RANK an INDEPENDENT DISTRIBUTOR had ever achieved within their active lifespan of their distributorship with that NETWORK MARKETING COMPANY'S

COMPENSATION PLAN; sometimes called Lifetime Rank. Once a distributor has achieved and QUALIFIED for a RANK, they may always be considered that RANK in title and RECOGNITION, even though they may not be paid at that RANK currently or in the future. The term itself refers to the practice that most COMPANIES continue to use within their RECOGNITION program where when a new RANK is achieved and small lapel pin is sent to the INDEPENDENT DISTRIBUTOR that indicates that they have achieved a new high RANK. With this behavior the INDEPENDENT DISTRIBUTOR typically only wears, in order to be recognized, the highest RANK that they have ever achieved. Most marketing literature provided by the company and the INDEPENDENT DISTRIBUTORS, typically only reflects the PIN RANK of the INDEPENDENT DISTRIBUTORS. See also PAID RANK.

PLACEMENT- indicates the position a DISTRIBUTOR has been placed in an ORGANIZATION after the ENROLLMENT process. PLACEMENT can be, and usually is, separate from the SPONSOR relationship – placing a DISTRIBUTOR below another DISTRIBUTOR in an attempt to strategically build an ORGANIZATION. See also SPONSORING.

PLACEMENT TREE- a structure TREE which details the PLACEMENT of INDEPENDENT DISTRIBUTORS within an ORGANIZATION. This TREE can often be confused with the SPONSOR TREE or ENROLLMENT TREE, but has no direct connection within the actual ENROLLMENT or SPONSOR of the individual. The DISTRIBUTOR who SPONSORS will always retain that status in the SPONSOR TREE, but often times may have the freedom to place them in different ORGANIZATIONS within the PLACEMENT TREE. The PLACEMENT TREE is most often the TREE structure that the many of the primary BONUSES calculated off of (e.g. BINARY TREE, MATRIX TREE, or UNILEVEL TREE). In these structures, separated from the ENROLLMENT TREE (genealogy) DISTRIBUTORS can be strategically placed to adhere to structure requirements, to maximize RANK advancements or COMMISSIONS. The only standard rule with placement within the PLACEMENT TREE is that the PLACEMENT of the DISTRIBUTOR should be somewhere within the PLACEMENT organization of the SPONSORING DISTRIBUTOR. See also SPONSOR TREE.

POLICIES AND PROCEDURES- a binding document containing all the rules, regulations, and restrictions that a COMPANY has the power to enforce upon an INDEPENDENT DISTRIBUTOR and the potential consequences of DISTRIBUTOR violations. POLICIES AND PROCEDURES are always agreed upon at the time of ENROLLMENT by the INDEPENDENT DISTRIBUTOR usually through a clause of the DISTRIBUTOR AGREEMENT, at which point they are immediately subject to all terms and conditions therein. The POLICIES AND PROCEDURES will often document internal practices and legal requirement; they will dictate the limitations placed upon the DISTRIBUTOR in building their business, MARKETING their business or product, and any limitation in building or manipulating their business. POLICIES AND PROCEDURES are designed to protect the COMPANY from the liability of INDEPENDENT DISTRIBUTOR action, giving the COMPANY full right to enforce the policies as they deem fit. The COMPLIANCE DEPARTMENT usually is the home for all potential policy violation investigations. COMPANIES also have full disclosure in their right to change or alter the POLICIES AND PROCEDURES as they deem fit in light of current business practices, legal requirements, restrictions, or DISTRIBUTOR behavior.

POOLS- a COMMISSION BONUS in which a POOL of money (usually a percentage of SALES or VOLUME) is accumulated, and then

DISTRIBUTOR in portions or by shares to QUALIFIED participants. Refer to BONUS POOLS for full definition.

POTENTIAL- at term indicated the possibilities within a COMPENSATION PLAN, NETWORK MARKETING, a PRODUCT, or a COMPANY as a whole. Usually, this term is used as a marketing term to emphasize the power within something.

POWER LEG- term is a marketable attempt in WEAK LEG BINARIES of the STRONG LEG; the LEG that contains the most amount of VOLUME between the two LEGS of the BINARY ORGANIZATION, and therefore the LEG that is expected to be the most powerful in terms of activity and growth. Term is synonymous with STRONG LEG. See also PAY LEG.

PREFERRED CUSTOMER- a CUSTOMER TYPE within a NETWORK MARKETING COMPANY that identifies CUSTOMERS who have qualified for some type of preferred treatment. Often the QUALIFICATIONS in order to become a PREFERRED CUSTOMER are in relation to agreeing to a regular AUTOSHIP or achieving a level of regular purchases. The preferred treatments could result in free PRODUCT credits, a discount on PRODUCT, or even the ability to purchase the PRODUCT at WHOLESALE PRICE. PREFERRED CUSTOMER are not DISTRIBUTORS, and are not allowed to have the same rights and privileges, but do need to submit an application to the COMPANY. PREFERRED CUSTOMERS do not participate in the COMPENSATION PLAN or any other NETWORK MARKETING activities. Often PREFERRED CUSTOMER purchases also count towards the SPONSORING DISTRIBUTORS personal purchases. See also DISTRIBUTOR and CUSTOMER.

PREFERRED CUSTOMER PRICE – an optional PRICE TYPE used by some COMPANIES to add another tier in their pricing. COMPANIES who use PREFERRED CUSTOMER PRICING do so as a reward for those CUSTOMERS who achieve some level or ordering activity and therefore become considered a PREFERRED CUSTOMER (see PREFERRED CUSTOMER for more details in offered programs). PREFERRED CUSTOMER PRICE, when used, is often times priced directly in the middle of WHOLESALE and RETAIL PRICES. This offers a discount to the PREFERRED CUSTOMER, but still give the greatest discount to the INDEPENDENT DISTRIBUTOR, allows for PREFERRED CUSTOMER purchases to still have a roll in RETAIL COMMISSIONS (the difference in prices), and allows there to still be an incentive for the PREFERRED CUSTOMER to upgrade to become an INDEPENDENT DISTRIBUTOR to gain the better WHOLESALE PRICE. See also WHOLESALE PRICE and RETAIL PRICE.

PRODUCT- the direct item or service being offered within the transaction being proposed by a NETWORK MARKETING COMPANY. This is the item or service that is being MARKETED within the COMPANY'S MARKETING literature, and is the intent of each INDEPENDENT DISTRIBUTOR to sell or distribute. This is the direct PRODUCT or SERVICE of a proposed value that is being received for the exchange of currency or VOLUME. Examples of products within the NETWORK MARKETING industry are nutritional supplements, skin care, cleaning products, online services, many other intangible services of value, or anything object that is physically exchanged for its purchase. See also INDIRECT PRODUCT.

PRODUCT MEETING (TRAINING)- an EVENT with the intent to train or introduce a PRODUCT or SERVICE of a NETWORK MARKETING COMPANY to DISTRIBUTORS, individuals, or potential DISTRIBUTORS. See also OPPORTUNITY MEETING, and PARTY.

PRODUCT VOLUME (PV)- the amount of VOLUME that is credited to the purchase of a particular PRODUCT or SERVICE provided by a NETWORK MARKETING COMPANY. The amount usually also reflects (unless indicated by the COMPANY) the amount of COMMISSIONABLE VOLUME and QUALIFYING VOLUME that will be credited to the COMMISSION ENGINE as a result of the purchase of the PRODUCT or SERVICE. The sum of the PRODUCT VOLUME within a population of ORDERS is what generates TOTAL COMPANY COMMISSIONABLE VOLUME, ORGANIZATION VOLUME, GROUP VOLUME, or any other accumulated VOLUME is usually calculated from the population. Can be synonymous with PERSONAL VOLUME in some COMPANIES.

PROGRESSIVE GENERATIONS- see "GENERATIONS (PROGRESSIVE)"

PROMOTION- a limited time offering of PRODUCT or additional COMMISSION EARNINGS for a unique behavior designed to increase SALES or DISTRIBUTOR COMMISSIONS; a temporary INCENTIVE to do something specific. Often times PROMOTIONS are ran by COMPANIES to advertise a PRODUCT, decrease inventory, increase revenue, or temporarily change behavior. DISTRIBUTORS also run PROMOTIONS within their ORGANIZATIONS to do the same things. DISTRIBUTOR PROMOTIONS are very effective models of building CULTURE within an organization, rewarding behavior, and incentivizing growth.

QUALIFICATIONS- requirements set forth by the NETWORK MARKETING COMPANY and documented within their published COMPENSATION PLAN to achieve or earn a RANK, BONUS, COMMISSION, or RECOGNITION. QUALIFICATIONS are designed to promote a particular behavior; this is done through compensating or rewarding the desired behavior once it has been accomplished. That reward most commonly comes in the form of RECOGNITION, trips, and additional EARNINGS. The QUALIFICATIONS within a COMPENSATION PLAN, PROMOTION, or COMPANY program are at the heart of the behavior the corporate staff believes will generate the greatest amount of growth and duplication benefiting both the corporation as a whole and the DISTRIBUTOR FIELD. See also RANKS, COMPENSATION PLAN, and QUALIFICATION PERIOD.

QUALIFICATION PERIOD- the PERIOD of time pre-determined by the company in which VOLUME and STRUCTURE requirements used to determine COMMISSION, POOL, BONUS, and RANK QUALIFICATION are accumulated. Often times these run in conjunction and simultaneously with COMMISSION PERIODS.

QUALIFIED- a term which indicates that a DISTRIBUTOR has met all the QUALIFICATIONS for a particular BONUS within the COMPENSATION PLAN, and therefore they are QUALIFIED to RANK advance, or to earn a particular COMMISSION. The term 'QUALIFIED' can also be a slang term used in many NETWORK MARKETING COMPANIES to denote a specific QUALIFICATION. For example, in many BINARY COMPENSATION PLANS they are required to have one ACTIVE personally ENROLLED member on each side of their BINARY TREE; being "ACTIVE" would mean that they have accumulated their required PERSONAL VOLUME, but being "QUALIFIED" for these COMPANIES means that they have met the two ENROLLMENT and PLACEMENT requirement, and are therefore QUALIFIED to earn the BINARY COMMISSIONS.

QUALIFYING VOLUME (QV)- a type of VOLUME that is used within the COMMISSION ENGINE to calculated and compare the QUALIFICATION for RANK ACHIEVEMENTS. QUALIFYING VOLUME is most commonly synonymous with COMMISSIONABLE VOLUME, or is at least INDUSTRY STANDARD to be equal in most COMPENSATION PLANS; therefore are not necessarily identified within the marketing literature of the COMPENSATION PLAN. QUALIFYING VOLUME is the only VOLUME amount a COMMISSION ENGINE looks at in ORDER to identify and determine the RANKS qualified for. There are times when as a result of FAST START BONUSES, that COMMISSIONABLE VOLUME would be discounted for different BONUSES, but it is less likely that QUALIFYING VOLUME is discounted. Regardless of whether QUALIFYING VOLUME is documented or discussed openly by a NETWORK MARKETING COMPANY, all COMMISSION ENGINES calculate ranks in relation to these VOLUME number; each product is set up with both PV and QV as independent number – even though in most circumstances they are the same numbers. See also COMMISSIONABLE VOLUME, PERSONAL VOLUME, PRODUCT VOLUME, SALES VOLUME, and UNCOMMISSIONABLE VOLUME.

QUARTERLY COMMISSION- EARNINGS that are QUALIFIED for within the COMPENSATION PLAN and issued quarterly in the form of a COMMISSION payment. Usually QUARTERLY BONUSES are larger LEADERSHIP BONUSES calculated outside of the standard COMMISSIONS cycle determined by the COMPANY; and can include revenue sharing bonuses or LEADERSHIP POOLS when the COMMISSION PERIOD for that BONUS has been established to be paid at the end of each quarter. Other BONUSES within the same COMPENSATION PLAN may be paid using a more regular COMMISSION PERIOD cycle such as: MONTHLY COMMISSIONS and WEEKLY COMMISSIONS. Also see EARNINGS, COMMISSIONS, BONUSES, and YEARLY COMMISSION.

R

RANKS- a status of RECOGNITION or achievement within a COMPENSATION PLAN. Each COMPENSATION PLAN determines bench-marks of achievements known as RANK QUALIFICATIONS. These usually require the minimal QUALIFICATION of being ACTIVE (FOR BONUSES), but may also include other requirements such as SALES VOLUME minimums, ranking LEGS, personal ENROLLMENTS, or any other desired behavior. As DISTRIBUTORS reach these QUALIFICATIONS within a predetermine time frame, known as a QUALIFICATION PERIOD, they are recognized at such RANKS, and are given the respective RANK titles. RANK often determines the particular BONUSES which the DISTRIBUTOR is QUALIFIED to earn from; the higher the RANK, the more BONUSES they earn from. The highest RANK a DISTRIBUTOR has ever QUALIFIED for is known as the PIN RANK. The current RANK a DISTRIBUTOR is paid at for a particular COMMISSION PERIOD is known as a PAID RANK. See also QUALIFICATIONS and COMPENSATION PLAN.

RECRUITING BONUS (ILLEGAL)- is a BONUS that is paid to the ENROLLER of a new DISTRIBUTOR as a result of their ENROLLMENT in the COMPANY, and not on the SALE of PRODUCT. This type of BONUS is illegal in most states, and is seen as a part of a pyramid or ponzi scheme. If the primary INCENTIVE for a BONUS is to ENROLL or recruit new members to a COMPANY, and not to increase the actual SALES of PRODUCT, than that BONUS is a prime candidate for an illegal RECRUITING BONUS. Many international COMPANIES also have a problem with these types of BONUSES.

RECRUITING BONUS (SLANG)- this slang comment usually refers to FAST START BONUSES, where a DISTRIBUTOR is compensated for the ENROLLMENT of a new DISTRIBUTOR and their purchase of initial or first ordered PRODUCT. These BONUSES are not like the RECRUITING BONUSES (ILLEGAL) which the law is concerned with, as the COMMISSIONS are calculated not directly on the ENROLLMENT itself, but on the additional PRODUCT VOLUME purchased by the new DISTRIBUTOR.

REFERRAL- a synonymous term with ENROLLER or SPONSOR, as the individual who introduced another CUSTOMER or DISTRIBUTOR to the ORGANIZATION; can also refer to the act of suggesting something to someone.

REGIONAL EVENT- an EVENT or meeting designed to cater to a region or larger geographical area than a normal meeting or EVENT. These events are traditionally much larger and more impressive to attend than regular meetings (like PARTIES, OPPORTUNITY or PRODUCT MEETINGS), but are not comparable to yearly CONVENTIONS.

RENEWAL FEE- a regular or reoccurring fee to the DISTRIBUTOR for account maintenance or services provided. RENEWAL FEES are documented in the company's POLICIES AND PROCEDURES and when utilized are intended as a requirement for the DISTRIBUTORS account to remain ACTIVE (FOR ORDERING). Most commonly these are yearly or bi-yearly fees. RENEWAL FEES have become more popular with COMPANIES that outsource their MLM Software platforms to supplement the fees associated with those tools.

RESIDUAL BONUSES (OR COMMISSIONS)- a term used to denote a continued payout on an ORGANIZATION or team that has been built regardless of current or future building activity of the INDEPENDENT DISTRIBUTOR. Usually the RESIDUAL BONUSES are those BONUSES which would define the plan structure (e.g. BINARY BONUS, UNILEVEL BONUS, MATRIX BONUS); but can also be bonus that can continually pay COMMISSIONS over an extended period of time in relation to the network that has been built (e.g. MATCHING BONUS, LEADERSHIP BONUS).

RETAIL- the highest suggested price for a PRODUCT or SERVICE offered by a NETWORK MARKETING COMPANY usually offered to DIRECT SALE RETAIL CUSTOMERS. Refer to RETAIL PRICE for the complete definition. Also see RETAIL CUSTOMER.

RETAIL BONUS (OR COMMISSIONS)- a BONUS TYPE or EARNINGS usually referring to the profit earned when a DISTRIBUTOR purchases the product at WHOLESALE and resells the same product at RETAIL PRICE. RETAIL COMMISSIONS is the difference or mark up between those two prices in which the INDEPENDENT DISTRIBUTOR pockets or earns from that transaction. Many companies offer the ability to allow INDEPENDENT DISTRIBUTORS to enroll RETAIL CUSTOMERS directly with the COMPANY, placing the COMPANY in the direct line of taking, charging, shipping, and fulfilling the Independent DISTRIBUTOR'S CUSTOMER'S orders. In these circumstances, RETAIL COMMISSIONS can refer to the money retained by the COMPANY when charging the CUSTOMER full RETAIL PRICE, but that the INDEPENDENT DISTRIBUTOR would have earned if they had personally purchased the product at WHOLESALE PRICE and fulfilled the order themselves. When these EARNINGS are retained by the company they are issued directly to the INDEPENDENT DISTRIBUTOR within the next commission earnings cycle. See also RETAIL PRICE, WHOLESALE PRICE, and RETAIL CUSTOMERS.

RETAIL CUSTOMER- term used to refer to a CUSTOMER TYPE which purchases the SERVICES or PRODUCTS of a NETWORK MARKETING COMPANY at full RETAIL price. RETAIL CUSTOMERS do not participate in the COMPENSATION PLAN or any other NETWORK MARKETING activities. RETAIL CUSTOMERS often are required to be referred or SPONSORED by a DISTRIBUTOR, or even purchase at RETAIL price directly from them. Term is synonymous with CUSTOMER. See also PREFERRED CUSTOMER and DISTRIBUTOR.

RETAIL PRICE- a PRICE TYPE which reflects the suggested RETAIL PRICE for a company's PRODUCT or SERVICES. This is the price that RETAIL

CUSTOMERS pay, or that INDEPENDENT DISTRIBUTORS charge to their direct customers. The difference between RETAIL PRICE and WHOLESALE PRICE is a critical tool used in NETWORK MARKETING for a number of reasons. Often times this price difference between the two determines the profitability for the INDEPENDENT DISTRIBUTORS for RETAILING the product. The RETAIL PRICE can also be used indirectly to enroll other INDEPENDENT DISTRIBUTORS. The average mark up from WHOLESALE PRICE to RETAIL PRICE in NETWORK MARKETING is between 20% and 35%. See also WHOLESALE PRICE and PREFERRED CUSTOMER PRICE.

RETENTION- the rate, ratio, percentage or timeline of the lifespan of an ACTIVE INDEPENDENT DISTRIBUTOR. Often times refers to how many DISTRIBUTORS or CUSTOMERS regularly purchase PRODUCT after their initial ENROLLMENT, and within a particular timeline from that ENROLLMENT. The higher the retention rate, the more DISTRIBUTORS or CUSTOMERS remain actively purchasing the PRODUCT or SERVICES. In NETWORK MARKETING, retention not only increases SALES VOLUME for both the COMPANY and UPLINE DISTRIBUTORS, but also increases potential DUPLICATION within the ORGANIZATION. RETENTION is usually determined by determining the amount of DISTRIBUTORS who are still purchasing after a pre-determined period of time. Industry standards within CORPORATE environments, looks at the amount of DISTRIBUTORS still purchasing three months after enrollment for a baseline RETENTION number, and continues to look every six, nine, and twelve months. See also ATTRITION and ACTIVE (FOR BONUSES).

RETRACTION- the return of VOLUME, credit, or previously earned COMMISSIONS from an INDEPENDENT DISTRIBUTOR back to the COMPANY, usually as a result of RETURNS or returning product. As previously ORDERED and COMMISSIONED PRODUCT is returned to the COMPANY and that order is no longer considered a valid SALE, RETRACTIONS are the way that all COMMISSIONS, credit, or VOLUME that has been awarded as a result of that sale is pulled back to the COMPANY – rectifying the over payment of COMMISSIONS or credit because of the now invalid sale. As a standard rule of practice RETRACTIONS take place upon receipt of the returning PRODUCT, and its approval as a return (not at the time request of the RMA took place). RETRACTIONS are a necessary part of doing business within the NETWORK MARKETING INDUSTRY. As some companies may not process RETRACTIONS, or do them appropriately, they open themselves up to substantial COMMISSION MANIPULATION ultimately damaging the businesses of all INDEPENDENT DISTRIBUTORS within the COMPANY. RETRACTIONS can result in previously earned COMMISSIONS being requested to be returned to the COMPANY, VOLUME to be retracted from future PERIODS to be made up from future SALES, or EARNINGS being withheld from future earned COMMISSIONS. See also RETURNS, ORDERS, and COMMISSION MANIPULATION.

RETURN MERCHANDISE AUTHORIZATION (RMA)- confirmation number often required by a COMPANY in order to send back PRODUCT or have a RETURN ORDER processed successfully. Most COMPANIES require an RMA to be requested by the returning purchaser from the COMPANY the PRODUCT is being returned to. This requirement is often detailed in every POLICIES AND PROCEDURES, and ensures that every RETURN is tracked and credited back to the correct account. Without an RMA there is little or no guarantee that a returning ORDER will be able to be sourced back to the shipper and then traced back to the original account in order to process the return. For this reason RMAs are often requested or required to be received by calling into the CUSTOMER SERVICE DEPARTMENT, and then subsequently placed on the outside of the box so that the receiving warehouse can identify to whom it belongs. RMAs also guarantee any verbal agreement in relation to the RETURN between the DISTRIBUTOR and the CALL CENTER representative will be upheld – without which there would be no record that such an agreement is connected to the returning package. See also ORDERS and RETURNS.

RETURNS- collective term referring to ORDERS that have been requested, paid for, delivered, commissioned, and then subsequently returned to the COMPANY. RETURNS can directly affect future and past COMMISSIONS depending on what COMMISSIONS have been processed and paid for as a result of the original ORDER that is no longer valid; as an ORDER returns that ORDER is no longer considered a sale, in the present PERIOD, or in the PERIOD that it was originally requested for. When RETURNS are processed and received by the COMPANY it usually results in some form of VOLUME RETRACTION or COMMISSION RETRACTION through the ORGANIZATION of those who may have earned money or credit on the original ORDER; this takes place in the form of RETRACTIONS. Each company has its own return policy and they are agreed to by each INDEPENDENT DISTRIBUTOR through the application process, agreement to the DISTRIBUTOR AGREEMENT, or through the POLICIES AND PROCEDURES of the company. See also RETRACTION, ORDER, and RETURN MERCHANDISE AUTHORIZATION (RMA).

REWARDS PLAN- a marketing term that can be used to describe the COMPENSATION or COMMISSION PLAN of a COMPANY. Terms emphasizes the potentially rewarding life style that is often marketed within the NETWORK MARKETING INDUSTRY. Please see COMPENSATION PLAN for the full definition.

RIGHT LEG (BINARY)- refers to the RIGHT LEG in the BINARY ORGANIZATION. RIGHT LEGS refer to the right side of the ORGANIZATION as the DISTRIBUTOR is looking at the ORGANIZATION, not as if they are inside or looking down upon the ORGANIZATION. See also LEFT LEG BINARY.

RIGHT LEG (MATRIX)- refers to the RIGHT LEG in the MATRIX ORGANIZATION. RIGHT LEGS are to the right side of the ORGANIZATION as the DISTRIBUTOR is looking at the ORGANIZATION, not as if they are inside or looking down upon the ORGANIZATION. See also LEFT LEG (MATRIX) and CENTER LEG (MATRIX).

ROLL-UP (POSITIONS)- a form of PLACEMENT COMPRESSION in which the actual position of a DISTRIBUTOR can roll-up the TREE permanently in circumstances where there are vacant or INACTIVE positions. These are usually used within MATRIX PLANS, and allow the DISTRIBUTOR to slowly roll up the TREE and gain a greater position as other individuals leave the ORGANIZATION. This is uncommon in the INDUSTRY for a reason, and is often met with serious long term consequences.

ROLL-UP (VOLUME)- a form of COMPRESSION in which VOLUME rolls up the TREE to another QUALIFIED participate or DISTRIBUTOR. This can be in the form of a VOLUME COMPRESSION, where the VOLUME is COMPRESSED to another LEVEL of the ORGANIZATION to increase a DISTRIBUTOR'S COMMISSIONS. This can also be a term used to describe an OVERRIDE ROLL UP, where only part of the VOLUME is used in the QUALIFICATION or COMMISSIONS of a DISTRIBUTOR and all excess

VOLUME can ROLL UP to a more qualified DISTRIBUTOR through the UPLINE. This type of ROLL-UP is also designed to increase COMMISSION payout and RANK QUALIFICATIONS. See also OVERRIDE COMPRESSION, COMPRESSION, and OVERRIDE.

S

SALES DEPARTMENT- the corporate department responsible for managing the corporate sales working through the INDEPENDENT DISTRIBUTORS. Often this department manages EVENTS, trainings about NETWORK MARKETING or PRODUCT, PROMOTIONS, and attempt to incentivize growth and an increase of PRODUCT SALES. See also MARKETING DEPARTMENT, DISTRIBUTOR NETWORK SERVICES, and ELITE SERVICES.

SALES VOLUME- a type of VOLUME that indicates the actual revenue generated by an order or the accumulation of orders within an ORGANIZATION, GROUP, or COMPANY. This is usually the revenue in the local currency, and is often an independent figure than the COMMISSIONABLE VOLUME or QUALIFYING VOLUME generated from the same sales. SALES VOLUME is rarely emphasized in marketing material within NETWORK MARKETING, but his extremely emphasized within the corporate environment. The NETWORK MARKETING COMPANY cares about the SALES VOLUME that comes into the COMPANY (the cash which flows into the COMPANY), and most

INDEPENDENT DISTRIBUTORS are mostly concerned with the amount of COMMISSIONABLE VOLUME that is generated within their ORGANIZATION (the amount of VOLUME they will get credit for in calculating their COMMISSIONS). See also COMMISSIONABLE VOLUME, QUALIFYING VOLUME, PERSONAL VOLUME and PERSONAL VOLUME.

SERVICE- a key PRODUCT offered by a NETWORK MARKETING COMPANY that may be intangible, and is a regularly offered or received SERVICE provided by the company. Examples of a SERVICE PRODUCT may be similar to: cable service, online services, internet service, house cleaning, etc. See also PRODUCT.

SPONSOR- the parent or upline DISTRIBUTOR whom is or has personally introduced and SPONSORED the CHILD or DOWNLINE DISTRIBUTOR into the ORGANIZATION. The SPONSOR of a DISTRIBUTOR can carry with it certain responsibilities within many POLICIES AND PROCEDURES including, but not limited to the requirement to support and train personally SPONSORED DISTRIBUTORS. The SPONSOR of a DISTRIBUTOR also carries with it certain rights legally and within many POLICIES AND PROCEDURES, including, but not limited to: autonomy of PLACEMENT, right for continued communication outside of the policies and COMPANY supervision, first right for training program placements, and many more. Term can be synonymous with ENROLLER.

SPONSORED- the act of joining an ORGANIZATION or COMPANY, and having been ENROLLED by an ACTIVE (FOR ORDERING) member of that ORGANIZATION.

SPONSORING- the act of enrolling a new INDEPENDENT DISTRIBUTOR into the NETWORK MARKETING ORGANIZATION.

SPONSOR TREE- TREE which details the SPONSORING or ENROLLING activity of an INDEPENDENT DISTRIBUTOR and the DISTRIBUTORS within his personal SPONSOR TREE ORGANIZATION. SPONSOR TREES are usually always UNILEVEL TREES in that it detailed the genealogy of SPONSORING activity, and therefore can contain multiple LEGS (or personally ENROLLED connections), and unlimited LEVELS. The first LEVEL of the SPONSOR TREE will detail those who are directly SPONSORED by the INDEPENDENT DISTRIBUTOR regardless of PLACEMENT within any other TREE structure supported by the NETWORK MARKETING COMPANY. As those individuals on the first LEVEL of the SPONSOR TREE begin SPONSORING other DISTRIBUTORS themselves (their own first LEVEL), those new ENROLLMENTS are detailed as the second LEVEL of the original INDEPENDENT DISTRIBUTOR. There are many BONUSES and RANK requirements which may be calculated or determined by the SPONSOR TREE. Often times this is called the hidden TREE within many companies, as it is built in the background of the COMPANY and is build regardless of intent. Term can be synonymous with ENROLLMENT TREE. See also UNILEVEL TREE, BINARY TREE, MATRIX TREE, and TREE.

SPONSOR TREE VOLUME- the amount of total PRODUCT VOLUME accumulated throughout the entire SPONSOR TREE ORGANIZATION within a given COMMISSION or QUALIFICATION PERIOD. This volume sums the volume within all Sponsor Tree Legs. This can also refer to ORGANIZATION VOLUME within the respective SPONSOR TREE STRUCTURE. See also ENROLLMENT TREE VOLUME.

STACKING- usually a violation of a company's published POLICIES AND PROCEDURES, where the DISTRIBUTOR accounts within an ORGANIZATION is artificially built or 'stacked' to maximize

COMMISSIONS or BONUSES within the COMPENSATION PLAN. The key term is *artificially* built, which indicates manipulation of the COMPENSATION PLAN. A violation of this policy can be as small as strategically placing qualifying orders, or as large as building an entire ORGANIZATION through fraudulent ENROLLMENTS to generate additional COMMISSIONS. In most circumstances, each violation is identified through the COMMISSIONS DEPARTMENT, but enforced through the COMPLIANCE and legal department in relation to the violation. In many instances, these are considered theft from the CORPORATE office, and from the rest of the DISTRIBUTOR field. STACKING is usually identified within the COMPLIANCE DEPARTMENT through questionably structured ORGANIZATIONS, non-unique names, invalid government IDs, multiple accounts or orders with similar credit cards, all resulting in the increase of COMMISSIONS or BONUS payout. See also COMMISSION MANIPULATION and BONUS BUYING.

STAIR STEP BREAKAWAY- a COMPENSATION PLAN type which is generally based off of the achievements of ORGANIZATIONS as a whole. As an enrolled DISTRIBUTOR within another DISTRIBUTOR'S organization progresses through the COMPENSATION PLAN RANKS and QUALIFICATIONS the ORGANIZATION which they manage progressively removes themselves and their TEAM from their UPLINE'S ORGANIZATION, or "breaks away". These 'broken away' TEAMS or ORGANIZATIONS become TEAMS of their own with little or no influence from other UPLINE members.

STANDARD COMPRESSION- a type of COMPRESSION in which when an empty or INACTIVE POSITION is present within a TREE during a COMMISSION run, the first LEVEL or following LEVEL of that INACTIVE position is moved within that INACTIVE position for the purposes of COMMISSION payout, calculation or credit. See also DYNAMIC COMPRESSION (ORIGINAL), DYNAMIC COMPRESSION (COMPRESSED), and COMPRESSION.

STRONG LEG- a term used in BINARY STRUCTURES (usually WEAK LEG BINARIES) to describe the LEG that contains the most amount of VOLUME between the two LEGS of the BINARY ORGANIZATION. Term is synonymous with POWER LEG. See also WEAK LEG.

STRUCTURE BONUS- a BONUS calculated within the COMMISSION ENGINE the QUALIFICATIONS of which relate to fulfilling a predetermined or corporate presented structure within a DISTRIBUTORS GENEALOGY TREE or ORGANIZATION. STRUCTURE BONUSES usually contain requirement in relation to how an ORGANIZATION is built (visibly looks on the GENEALOGY TREE) within an outlined structure, the fulfillment of which generates a particular COMMISSION or EARNING. Examples of STRUCTURE BONUSES would be similar to: If a DISTRIBUTOR ORGANIZATION has X people on their first LEVEL, and Y people on their second LEVEL all purchasing at a specific dollar or VOLUME amount — than the COMPANY will issue an additional BONUS of cash above and beyond all other BONUSES only because the structure was completed as requested. STRUCTURE BONUSES are usually the most manipulated in regard to BONUS BUYING and STACKING activities, in an effort to maximize DISTRIBUTOR EARNINGS; and therefore is usually or should be the most monitored within the CORPORATE ENVIRONMENT.

STRUCTURE TYPE- refers to the category of building requirements and structure that will be enforced within a major component or BONUS of the COMPENSATION PLAN provided by the NETWORK MARKETING COMPANY. These STRUCTURE TYPES define what the rules, expectations, and guidelines that will determine what will be enforced upon the INDEPENDENT DISTRIBUTOR in how they build their GENEALOGY or ORGANIZATION TREE for any RESIDUAL BONUSES or COMMISSIONS. There are traditionally three major structures that define the type of COMPENSATION PLAN that are commonly referred to within the NETWORK MARKETING INDUSTRY: BINARY, MATRIX, and UNILEVEL. There are also other STRUCTURE TYPES that are in the INDUSTRY that are not as well known, but often highly publicized for short periods of time – but those three STRUCTURE TYPES are the most commonly used and tested throughout the INDUSTRY.

SUSPENDED- a status which indicates a temporary hold on the rights and available actions of the INDEPENDENT DISTRIBUTOR in relation to building their business. Such temporary holds are usually the result of an ongoing or pending investigation regarding COMPLIANCE or any potential violations of company policy as dictated by the company's POLICIES AND PROCEDURES. At the conclusion of such investigations the SUSPENDED account is then either restored to ACTIVE (FOR ORDERING) or is TERMINATED, depending on the results. Holds can include: current or future COMMISSIONS, rights to ENROLL, access to the BACK OFFICE and organizational data, access to communicate with their ORGANIZATION, and even the right to purchase additional PRODUCT.

T

TAXABLE EARNINGS- the total amount of EARNINGS generated by a DISTRIBUTOR for which the local, state, or federal government requires are stated in past, current, or future tax documents. All COMMISSIONS with rare exceptions are considered TAXABLE EARNINGS, and are should be reported to the local and federal government for income declaration. See also TEN NINETY-NINE (1099).

TEAM- refers to a group of people or ACTIVE DISTRIBUTORS. Term may be used to describe a population within an ORGANIZATION, a population under and leading DISTRIBUTOR, a population within a structured LEG, or a population within a shared community.

TEN NINETY-NINE (1099)- legal document issued for United State residents which detail the INDEPENDENT DISTRIBUTOR'S TAXABLE EARNINGS for a calendar tax year. This document is required to be generated and sent to the DISTRIBUTORS every year by January 31st for the previous tax year, and generally includes the account name, address, Social Security Number or other Tax Identification Numbers (EIN), TAXABLE EARNINGS for the year, and total PRODUCT purchases for the year. 1099's are only required to be issued by the NETWORK MARKETING COMPANY to the DISTRIBUTORS in event that the DISTRIBUTOR has earned over $600 USD, or has purchased in excess $5,000 USD of PRODUCT for the tax year. In circumstances where a 1099 is not issued, the DISTRIBUTOR is still liable to report any TAXABLE EARNINGS to the governing tax agency. See also TAXABLE EARNINGS.

TERMINATED- status of a DISTRIBUTOR account which indicated that the account has been permanently closed, and therefore has no current rights or privileges offered by the company including, but not limited to the ability to ORDER, recruit, ENROLL, earn COMMISSIONS, represent the COMPANY, retail the PRODUCT, or participate in corporate sponsored PROMOTIONS or EVENTS. This status is often a result of voluntary TERMINATION, unpaid renewal fees, or the result of a COMPLIANCE investigation. See also ACTIVE (FOR ORDERING), SUSPENDED, CANCELLED, and INACTIVE (FOR ORDERING).

"THE LIST"- a commonly used activity in identifying and documenting an INDEPENDENT DISTRIBUTOR'S WARM MARKET. Many SPONSORS request or encourage that members of their ORGANIZATION create a list of their WARM MARKET including: friends, family, associates, neighbors, co-workers, and everyone that they can think of that they have a neutral or positive relationship with. This list is used to help each INDEPENDENT DISTRIBUTOR identify potential CUSTOMERS or those interested in becoming INDEPENDENT DISTRIBUTORS themselves. After making the list the INDEPENDENT DISTRIBUTOR is then encouraged to contact as many people on that LIST as possible and inform them of the COMPANY, PRODUCT, or OPPORTUNITY through a MEETING, presentation, CONFERENCE CALL, WEBINAR, or any other activity that might be conducive to generating interest within these individuals. See also WARM MARKET.

TOTAL COMPANY COMMISSIONABLE VOLUME (TCCV)- the sum or grand total of a COMPANY'S global COMMISSIONABLE VOLUME generated, sold, or purchased within a determined PERIOD of time, usually a COMMISSION or QUALIFICATION PERIOD. TCCV is usually used in the calculation of BONUSES that are usually offered to the entire company globally. See also TOTAL MARKET COMMISSIONABLE VOLUME (TMCV), and SALES VOLUME.

TOTAL MARKET COMMISSIONABLE VOLUME (TMCV)- the sum or grand total of a market's COMMISSIONABLE VOLUME (domestic or international) generated, sold, or purchased within a determined PERIOD of time, usually a COMMISSION or QUALIFICATION PERIOD. TMCV is usually used in the calculation of BONUSES that may be specific to a particular market. See also TOTAL COMPANY COMMISSIONABLE VOLUME (TCCV), and SALES VOLUME.

TREE- is a generic term which refers to the structure of the genealogy of ENROLLMENTS or PLACEMENT within the COMPANY or ORGANIZATION. The respective TREE contains all of the relationships involved. Often the type of TREE is connected to the type of structure the COMPENSATION PLAN promotes (e.g. BINARY TREE, MATRIX TREE, ENROLLMENT TREE, UNILEVEL TREE, etc.). The TREE also details the relationships which can often define the potential of COMMISSIONS that can be earned and from whom, the QUALIFICATION and REQUIREMENTS for RANKS, and how the ORGANIZATION can grow with respect to the type of structure the COMPENSATION PLAN promotes. The respective TREE can usually be viewed through a VIRTUAL OFFICE that may be offered by the COMPANY. Anything that details the genealogy can be considered a TREE, and is called such because when mapped out visually including all connected relationships between the individuals (UPLINE and DOWNLINE) the image can be compared to the image of a TREE, root and branch systems, or traditional family history TREE. The TREE is also used to indicate volume flow and credit throughout the ORGANIZATION.

UNCOMMISSIONABLE PRODUCT- a PRODUCT or SERVICE that does not carry with it any COMMISSIONABLE VOLUME, and therefore the SALE or purchases of the PRODUCT will not issue or generate any COMMISSIONS, EARNINGS, or aid in QUALIFICATIONS within the COMPENSATION PLAN.

UNCOMMISSIONABLE VOLUME- SALES VOLUME that does not carry with it any COMMISSIONABLE VOLUME that will generate COMMISSIONS or EARNINGS. The SALES of PRODUCT or SERVICES that do not generate any COMMISSIONS is considered to be UNCOMMISSIONABLE VOLUME. Usually, as a result of legal concerns, the actual SALES generated from the ENROLLMENT itself within a NETWORK MARKETING COMPANY is considered to be UNCOMMISSIONABLE VOLUME, while the PRODUCT purchased at the time of ENROLLMENT would be classified as carrying COMMISSIONABLE VOLUME. See also DISCOUNTED VOLUME.

UNCOMMON LEG- a LEG that is not shared directly with an immediate UPLINE SPONSOR or PLACEMENT. Term is most commonly relevant within BINARY ORGANIZATIONS. This is any LEG or LEGS that are not considered to be the COMMON LEG, and are usually expected to be built directly by the INDEPENDENT DISTRIBUTOR with little or no support.

UNILEVEL (STRUCTURE)- a STRUCTURE TYPE which has the least degree of enforced structure. A UNILEVEL can have as many LEGS, and as many levels in depth as the INDEPENDENT DISTRIBUTOR can build or acquire. Unlike other structures there is nothing that requires the PLACEMENT of SPONSORED members within another's personal TEAM. Within the UNILEVEL each direct connection (either through sponsorship or placement) to an INDEPENDENT DISTRIBUTOR is considered a new leg. The UNILEVEL term is derived from the original notion of MULTI-LEVEL MARKETING where the emphasis is that through NETWORK MARKETING DISTRIBUTORS gain multiple levels of other DISTRIBUTORS within their ORGANIZATION. Most common variations within the UNILEVEL structure is the type of COMPRESSION that is used within the COMPENSATION PLAN. See also STRUCTURE TYPE, BINARY, and MATRIX.

UNILEVEL BONUS- a BONUS within the COMPENSATION PLAN which pays off of the STRUCTURE, VOLUME, or DISTRIBUTOR activity within the UNILEVEL TREE of an INDEPENDENT DISTRIBUTOR. This can include BONUSES which pay specific to LEG VOLUME or LEVEL VOLUME within the UNILEVEL TREE. All BONUSES that are paid in relation to the UNILEVEL ORGANIZATION or TREE is considered a UNILEVEL BONUS regardless of whether they pay per LEVEL, GENERATION, or with COMPRESSION. Many QUALIFICATIONS or REQUIREMENTS in order to earn UNILEVEL BONUSES can include personally ACTIVE (FOR BONUS) DISTRIBUTORS within the ORGANIZATION, number of QUALIFIED LEGS within the ORGANIZATION at a particular RANK (LEG RANK), or the

QUALIFIED PAID RANK for the INDEPENDENT DISTRIBUTOR. These usually are considered a RESIDUAL BONUS of a COMPENSATION PLAN with a UNILEVEL TREE attached. Other BONUSES based off of the STRUCTURE TYPE of the COMPENSATION PLAN are BINARY BONUS and MATRIX BONUS. See also RECRUITING BONUS, FAST START BONUS, STRUCTURE BONUS, and MATCHING BONUS.

UNILEVEL COMMISSIONS- refers to EARNINGS or COMMISSIONS of an INDEPENDENT DISTRIBUTOR which is earned from any UNILEVEL BONUSES that were QUALIFIED for and offered within the COMPENSATION PLAN. This can commonly be referred to as a RESIDUAL COMMISSION; similar to UNILEVEL COMMISSIONS and MATRIX COMMISSIONS. See also COMMISSIONS, EARNINGS, and COMMISSIONS PAYMENTS.

UNILEVEL LEGS- refers to the separate ORGANIZATIONS which are directly connected to an INDEPENDENT DISTRIBUTOR within a UNILEVEL STRUCTURE. Each individual directly placed or SPONSORED by an INDEPENDENT DISTRIBUTOR on a UNILEVEL STRUCTURE, would begin and be at the top of a LEG. The nature of the UNILEVEL STRUCTURE allows for any INDEPENDENT DISTRIBUTOR to have an un-limited amount of LEGS, determined only by the amount of personally SPONSORED or personally PLACED TEAM members within the ORGANIZATION. The amount of UNILEVEL LEGS and their poten-tial RANKS or achievements may be QUALIFICATIONS within the published COMPENSATION PLAN for RANK ADVANCEMENT.

UNILEVEL TREE- TREE which details the genealogical or ORGANIZATIONAL relationship of ENROLLMENTS or PLACEMENTS within the confines of a UNILEVEL structure. UNILEVEL TREES can refer to the PLACEMENTS of the DISTRIBUTORS within an ORGANIZATION, or the

ENROLLING activities, relationships, and genealogy of the ORGANIZATION (see ENROLLMENT TREE). As with the nature of the UNILEVEL structure, the UNILEVEL TREE details the structure of unlimited LEGS and the relationship in terms of LEVELS (or LEVELS of distance between each DISTRIBUTOR). Usually, new ENROLLMENTS are placed anywhere within any ORGANIZATION, LEG, or TEAM within the DOWNLINE of the ENROLLING DISTRIBUTOR. The main units of consideration within the UNILEVEL TREE is: (1) PLACEMENT of new ENROLLMENTS within LEGS and LEVELS of depth from the ENROLLER, (2) each level's relationship and comparison with the other LEVELS of the structure, (3) each LEG rank or VOLUME in relation and comparison with the other LEGS of the structure for the purpose of RANK QUALIFICATIONS and COMMISSIONS, (4) and the PLACEMENT of team member within the TREE. UNILEVEL TREES can have multiple LEGS and multiple levels. UNILEVEL BONUSES are determined by the VOLUME and activity that takes place within a particular LEVEL or GENERATION of the UNILEVEL TREE. See also TREE, BINARY TREE, ENROLLMENT TREE, SPONSOR TREE, and MATRIX TREE.

UNILEVEL TREE VOLUME- the amount of total PRODUCT VOLUME accumulated throughout the entire UNILEVEL TREE ORGANIZATION within a given COMMISSION or QUALIFICATION PERIOD. This VOLUME sums the VOLUME within all UNILEVEL TREE LEGS. This can also refer to ORGANIZATION VOLUME within the respective UNILEVEL STRUCTURE.

UPLINE- the individual to whom an INDEPENDENT DISTRIBUTOR is directly placed under or SPONSORED by. When referring to a group of people, this refers to the group of people or the line of GENEALOGY moving up the ORGANIZATIONAL TREE. UPLINE DISTRIBUTORS of an individual INDEPENDENT DISTRIBUTOR indicates that the UPLINE DISTRIBUTORS have an opportunity to earn a COMMISSION on the actions or behavior of the INDEPENDENT DISTRIBUTOR. UPLINE refers to those individuals with whom the INDEPENDENT DISTRIBUTOR has been placed or SPONSORED within their ORGANIZATION, and essentially are known as their UPLINE'S DOWNLINE. See also DOWNLINE.

VIRTUAL OFFICE- see BACK OFFICE for full definition.

VOLUME- is an overarching term often used to indicate an amount of credit or SALES that are accumulated, whether personally or through an ORGANIZATION. There are many different terms and types of VOLUME all used for very different purposes, and used in many different calculation processes with a NETWORK MARKETING COMPANY and the COMPENSATION PLAN. VOLUME types indicate the type of credit accumulated from the purchase of the COMPANY'S PRODUCT or SERVICES. Examples of the types of VOLUME associated with many NETWORK MARKETING COMPANIES are: COMMISSIONABLE VOLUME, QUALIFYING VOLUME, PRODUCT VOLUME, PERSONAL VOLUME, and SALES VOLUME. VOLUME can also be referring to a pool of VOLUME of any one type, as related to a STRUCTURE or ORGANIZATION. Examples of Volume Pools often used with NETWORK MARKETING COMPANIES are: TOTAL COMPANY COMMISSIONABLE VOLUME, ORGANIZATION VOLUME, LEG

VOLUME, RIGHT LEG VOLUME, LEFT LEG VOLUME, GROUP VOLUME, and LEVEL VOLUME. VOLUME types typically are the units which comprise the Volume Pools. All calculated volumes within a published COMPENSATION PLAN are usually used for QUALIFICATION, tracking, or COMMISSION purposes. There are also terms which are related to the type of VOLUME or lack therefore, such as: UNCOMMISSIONABLE VOLUME, FLUSHED VOLUME, CARRY OVER VOLUME, and DISCOUNTED VOLUME.

WARM MARKET- a term used in the NETWORK MARKETING INDUSTRY to denote an INDEPENDENT DISTRIBUTOR'S known associates or contacts from their day to day experiences. A WARM MARKET is an INDEPENDENT DISTRIBUTOR'S friends, co-workers, family, neighbors, and any other associates from whom there may be a warm relationship with that the INDEPENDENT DISTRIBUTOR may feel more comfortable approaching concerning a PRODUCT or OPPORTUNITY. A WARM MARKET is most commonly used in the process of creating "THE LIST" that many networkers encourage their ORGANIZATIONS to do. This is opposed to a COLD MARKET.

WEAKER LEG BINARY- a COMPENSATION PLAN model from the BINARY STRUCTURE TYPE; COMPENSATION is generally determined in relation to the amount of VOLUME within the COMMISSION PERIOD contained within the WEAK LEG, or the lesser of the two LEGS when comparing the two LEGS of the BINARY ORGANIZATION. WEAKER LEG BINARIES pay a predetermined COMMISSION percentage from the VOLUME accumulated in the WEAK LEG of the ORGANIZATION. The more VOLUME generated within the WEAK LEG of the BINARY ORGANIZATION, the more COMMISSIONS that are earned from the ORGANIZATION. WEAKER LEG BINARIES often are used to require a more balanced perspective between the two LEGS, encouraging the ORGANIZATION to be built in an attempt to balance the VOLUME between the two LEGS in order to maximize the potential COMMISSIONS in the BINARY BONUS. WEAKER LEG BINARIES are stable only when there are conservative EARNING LIMITATIONS on the BINARY BONUS. When the WEAKER LEG is used to generate COMMISSIONS in the BINARY BONUS, the total amount of VOLUME used to generate those commissions is then FLUSHED from both LEGS of the BINARY. The concept that only the VOLUME in the WEAK LEG is paid on has generated some legal issues within the INDUSTRY; yet, this action of paying on only the WEAK LEG VOLUME within WEAKER LEG BINARIES, is more of a marketing illusion in an effort to keep the BINARY BONUS or COMMISSIONS simple to understand. Although, WEAKER LEG BINARIES are simple because of the way they pay a percentage from the WEAK LEG, in an effort to legitimize the STRUCTURE TYPE, they really pay half of the marketed percentage on both legs of the BINARY, down to the depth of the WEAKEST LEG; this also justifies the VOLUME FLUSH that takes place in both legs of the WEAKER LEG BINARY. Other COMPENSATION PLAN models from the BINARY STRUCTURE are: HYBRID BINARY and CYCLE BINARY.

WEAK LEG- a term used in BINARY STRUCTURES (usually WEAK LEG BINARIES) to describe the LEG that contains the least amount of

VOLUME between the two LEGS of the BINARY ORGANIZATION. Term is synonymous with PAY LEG and LESSER LEG. See also STRONG LEG.

WEBINAR- a virtual tool used by many INDEPENDENT DISTRIBUTOR in the NETWORK MARKETING INDUSTRY to build their business. A WEBINAR allows for a conference of people to view a presentation over the internet and allow as few or as many people to view the presentation wherever they are in the world. WEBINARS have become exceedingly popular over the decade in both the CORPORATE ENVIRONMENT and the DISTRIBUTOR field. See also CONFERENCE CALL.

WEEKLY COMMISSION- EARNINGS that are qualified for within the COMPENSATION PLAN and issued weekly in the form of a COMMISSION payment. Usually can include FAST START BONUS, or RESIDUAL BONUS EARNINGS when the COMMISSION PERIOD for that BONUS has been established by the company as a WEEKLY COMMISSION PERIOD cycle. Other COMMISSION PERIOD cycles which may be used for BONUSES include: MONTHLY COMMISSIONS, YEARLY COMMISSIONS, and QUARTERLY COMMISSIONS. Also see EARNINGS, COMMISSIONS, and BONUSES.

WHOLESALE- lowest price a PRODUCT or SERVICES are available to be PURCHASED; usually associated with the PRICE TYPE offered to the COMPANY'S INDEPENDENT DISTRIBUTORS. See WHOLESALE PRICE for full definition.

WHOLESALE DISTRIBUTOR- a term used by some NETWORK MARKETING COMPANIES for an INDEPENDENT DISTRIBUTOR. These companies use this term in an effort to emphasis the PRICE TYPE the DISTRIBUTOR qualifies for focusing on the value that is associated with joining the company as an INDEPENDENT DISTRIBUTOR. Refer to INDEPENDENT DISTRIBUTOR for full definition; also synonymous with INDEPENDENT PRODUCT CONSULTANT (IPC), INDEPENDENT BUSINESS OWNER (IBO) and ASSOCIATE. See also DISTRIBUTOR.

WHOLESALE PRICE- a PRICE TYPE that is offered to a NETWORK MARKETING COMPANY'S INDEPENDENT DISTRIBUTORS. This is often the lowest price available, allowing the INDEPENDENT DISTRIBUTOR to receive the largest discount on PRODUCT, and have the OPPORTUNITY to RETAIL the PRODUCT in turn receiving the largest profit from the resale of the PRODUCT or SERVICES provided by the COMPANY. Often times because of the significance between the WHOLESALE PRICE and RETAIL PRICE, many product users become INDEPENDENT DISTRIBUTORS only to receive the WHOLESALE PRICE (therefore creating an INDIRECT PRODUCT). See also RETAIL PRICE and PREFERRED CUSTOMER PRICE.

YEARLY COMMISSION- EARNINGS that are QUALIFIED for within the COMPENSATION PLAN and issued yearly in the form of a COMMISSION payment. Usually YEARLY COMMISSIONS include larger LEADERSHIP BONUSES which could be revenue sharing bonuses or LEADERSHIP POOLS when the COMMISSION PERIOD for that BONUS has been established to be paid at the end of the year. Other BONUSES within the same COMPENSATION PLAN may be paid out in relation to a more regularly COMMISSION PERIOD cycle, such as: WEEKLY COMMISSIONS, MONTHLY COMMISSIONS, and QUARTERLY COMMISSIONS. Also see EARNINGS, COMMISSIONS, and BONUSES.

Acknowledgments

The following individuals and companies have contributed in some way either through inspiration, support, or through lending experience to the author. More will be added to this section in future editions – please see "The Respectful Challenge" at the beginning of this work.

Robert Coombs

Young Living Essential Oils

Brittani Lambert

David Brieter

Genesis PURE

Daren Hogge

Reggie Rappleye

doTerra

Paparazzi

Trent and Misty Kirby

Daren Falter

Robby Fender

Yoli

Kyani

Adam Daley

Haylie Hoglund

Marcella Vonn Harting

Vicki Opfer

Cherie Ross

Bruce Bishop

About the Author

Ryan Daley is considered to be one of the most sought after corporate consultants within the network marketing industry. Using a combination of his experience through consulting with networkers, corporate executives, and in running, writing, and managing compensation plans, in conjunction with his education and study of behavior – he has developed a unique perspective and ability to see the industry in a holistic setting.

When receiving his Associates in Behavioral Science, Ryan was honored as the Valedictorian; he also graduated Summa Cum Laude with his Bachelors in Psychology from Utah Valley University. Ryan also studied for his Masters of Business Administration at the University of Utah, while continuing his research on the *psychology of sales in an incentive based environment (network marketing).*

Ryan has consulted directly with some of the largest leaders and earners within the network marketing industry, teaching them how to maximize their earnings within their respective compensation plan. He has developed many compensation plans, adjusted even more of them to gain stability, and managed the development of many commission engine implementations through a number of software packages. Using his experience he has also directly consulted with numerous network marketing companies to aid in turning around or adjusting distributor behavior and increasing sales and company stability. He currently is a Vice President of one of the fastest growing network marketing companies in history.

Ryan is married with two children, and loves his family.

103